"For everything that was written in the past was written to teach us, so that through the endurance taught in the Scriptures and the encouragement they provide we might have hope.

May the God who gives endurance and encouragement give you the same attitude of mind toward each other that Christ Jesus had, so that with one mind and one voice you may glorify the God and Father of our Lord Jesus Christ."

Romans 15:4-6

Graphic Design and Layout : Mélissa Caron — Enki Communications — Go-Enki.com

Edited by Allison Watkins

First Edition, 2011

First Printing, 2012

ISBN 978-1-908567-30-7

Women
of Courage
31 Daily Bible Readings

The Remarkable Untold Stories,
Challenges & Triumphs
Of Thirty-One Ordinary,
Yet Extraordinary, Bible Women

Introduction

In this devotional, through daily Bible readings, we will be looking at the stories and lives of thirty-one women in the Bible.

Each of these women has much to teach us. They each faced their own challenges, lived through shame and pain, yet learnt, through their trials, to place their trust in God. We will see how they can inspire us to be more courageous in our own lives.

As women, we work hard and live busy lives, often finding it difficult to rest and relax. Our hard work do often goes unnoticed or under-appreciated, as we quietly serve behind the scenes. We have a crucial role to play, but we can be unsure just what a godly woman looks like and how we can find the time become one!

As you read through these stories of ordinary, yet incredibly courageous women, I hope that you will find inspiration. You will see that each had a special calling for her time and place in history. You will see God shaping their characters, preparing them for their unique roles.

My prayer is that you will see how each of these women were very different, yet they each fit into God's story perfectly, like pieces in a jigsaw puzzle. Each of them reflected Godly qualities, yet each was unique in her own way.

In the same way, God has a unique plan and purpose for your life. You are created uniquely to be you. God has a special calling on your life, something that is tailored especially for your personality.

By trying to fit in the mould of any particular Bible character, or the person you feel you should become, you could miss out on God's best for you. Trying to be someone you're not can lead to frustration and bitterness, rather than following His plan, in which you will discover the fruitfulness and joy He has for you. Embracing it can lead to the joy and fulfillment that you've always hoped for and dreamed of.

I invite you to join me as we explore His plans and purposes for these thirty-one women. As we do so, I trust that God will reveal more of His plans and purposes for your life.

Table of Contents

Overcoming Shame and Pain

As Jesus was on his way, the crowds almost crushed him. And a woman was there who had been subject to bleeding for twelve years, but no one could heal her. She came up behind him and touched the edge of his cloak, and immediately her bleeding stopped.

"Who touched me?" Jesus asked. When they all denied it, Peter said, "Master, the people are crowding and pressing against you."

But Jesus said, "Someone touched me; I know that power has gone out from me."

Then the woman, seeing that she could not go unnoticed, came trembling and fell at his feet. In the presence of all the people, she told why she had touched him and how she had been instantly healed. Then he said to her, "Daughter, your faith has healed you. Go in peace."

Luke 8:42-48

How many times should we pray for healing before quitting? Once? Twice? Ten times? A hundred? After repeatedly asking for prayer, wouldn't you begin to feel a little self-conscious or embarrassed? Perhaps twinges of discouragement or cynicism would creep into your heart, causing you to doubt God's promises and wonder whether He truly cares for you.

Most of us have something in our lives that we're ashamed of, something we want to hide, something we're thankful our church friends don't know. What if that hidden sin was public knowledge, laid bare for all your neighbors and friends to see? What if you couldn't hide your shameful thoughts or actions anymore?

That is how this woman must have felt. For years, she sought healing in vain. She had spent all of her money on doctors who couldn't help. In Jewish culture, she was considered unclean; her neighbors saw her constant bleeding as a shameful condition. Through the years, friends and family probably ostracized her, leaving her feeling isolated. People likely whispered that some secret sin must be causing her suffering.

Yet she hadn't given up hope. She still had just enough faith, (though it may have been as small as a mustard seed), to push through the crowd that surrounded Jesus. In her condition, she shouldn't have been amidst the crowd at all, but she defied convention to come to Jesus.

She didn't dare try to get his attention, lest she draw attention to her shameful self. And what if He, too, turned her away? She couldn't bear to be rejected again, yet she knew deep down that Jesus was someone special — that somehow, just by getting close to Him, her life could be changed. And so, in an act of desperation, she reached out and touched the edge of His cloak as He passed by.

His power healed her immediately. But even when she took His power without His permission, Jesus didn't turn from her as everyone else had. In His words, "Daughter, your faith has healed you, go in peace," He told her the three things that she had so longed to hear: She was accepted as a daughter, she was healed and she would finally experience peace.

After years of living in shame, she finally experienced acceptance. For the first time since she was a girl, she was free to live a normal life. Finally, she knew the peace that she sought for so many years.

Jesus is the same yesterday, today and forever. He is still the One who desires to restore you from years of pain, shame and discouragement. He wants to heal the places where you ache physically and emotionally.

Is there something that you're remembering, even now, that makes you feel ashamed or that you want to hide? After all this time spent living with it, why not bring your pain or shame to Jesus and ask Him to touch and change your life?

Generosity in Desperate Times

Then the word of the Lord came to Elijah: "Leave here, turn eastward and hide in the Kerith Ravine, east of the Jordan. You will drink from the brook, and I have directed the ravens to supply you with food there."

So he did what the Lord had told him. He went to the Kerith Ravine, east of the Jordan, and stayed there. The ravens brought him bread and meat in the morning and bread and meat in the evening, and he drank from the brook. Some time later the brook dried up because there had been no rain in the land.

Then the word of the Lord came to him: "Go at once to Zarephath in the region of Sidon and stay there. I have directed a widow there to supply you with food."

So he went to Zarephath. When he came to the town gate, a widow was there gathering sticks. He called to her and asked, "Would you bring me a little water in a jar so I may have a drink?" As she was going to get it, he called, "And bring me, please, a piece of bread."

"As surely as the Lord your God lives," she replied, "I don't have any bread—only a handful of flour in a jar and a little olive oil in a jug. I am gathering a few sticks to take home and make a meal for myself and my son, that we may eat it — and die."

Elijah said to her, "Don't be afraid. Go home and do as you have said. But first make a small loaf of bread for me from what you have and bring it to me, and then make something for yourself and your son. For this is what the Lord, the God of Israel, says: 'The jar of flour will not be used up and the jug of oil will not run dry until the day the Lord sends rain on the land.'"

She went away and did as Elijah had told her. So there was food every day for Elijah and for the woman and her family. For the jar of flour was not used up and the jug of oil did not run dry, in keeping with the word of the Lord spoken by Elijah.

1 Kings 17:2-16

What would you choose to eat for your last meal on earth? Maybe your favorite pizza, a carefully prepared meal from an expensive restaurant or a giant chocolate bar. Whatever your choice, it is probably fancier than a flat piece of bread made from flour and oil.

In 1 Kings, we read of a time of severe famine when the prophet Elijah came to a widow and her son just as she reached the end of her hope. Elijah found her gathering a few sticks to cook one final meal for herself and her son before they waited to die of hunger. She had run out of food and had no money to buy more.

We often see the details of our circumstances clearly, but fail to see how they fit into the bigger picture. Trusting God and His promises with our problems seems impossible, so we dwell on our situations rather than putting our faith in a truly almighty God. But God promises to provide for all our needs. His Word says:

"And my God will meet all your needs
according to the riches of his glory in Christ Jesus."

Philippians 4:19

This single mother and her son were blessed because of their obedience and generosity in the midst of hardship. Just as the Israelites had to depend on God for their daily manna and quail in the desert, this widow learned that dependence on God is a beautiful reality.

She didn't seem to know who Elijah was, yet something in her responded to his request for food. Perhaps it was the authority in his voice, or maybe she had simply accepted her dim fate, and nothing mattered to her anymore. Whichever, she was unbelievably generous to share her last few bites of food with a stranger. Despite a difficult season, she chose to remain faithful to her principles of generosity and hospitality. Her faith was rewarded, Elijah promised that her flour and oil would last until the end of the drought. She and her son lived, because of the miraculous provision of God.

In a society where we are used to feeling like we control our own lives, this passage may surprise us. We believe that our belongings are ours to use for our own families, and sharing is uncommon even within the church.

How many mothers would give away food if their children were hungry and the store shelves were bare? It seems illogical, doesn't it? It's certainly counter-cultural. We're so used to having more than enough that many of us have never truly learned what it is to trust God to provide what we need. Yet sometimes God will lead us to this place to teach us to trust Him, to rely on His provision and to experience the wonder of His love.

This widow learned to love a daily dependence on God. This was a beautiful experience for her because each day she was reminded of how much she was loved.

Is there something you need to trust God with today? Is God asking you to share or give away some of your resources to bless others?

Seeing the Bigger Picture in Challenging Circumstances

Now Naaman was commander of the army of the king of Aram. He was a great man in the sight of his master and highly regarded, because through him the Lord had given victory to Aram. He was a valiant soldier, but he had leprosy. Now bands of raiders from Aram had gone out and had taken captive a young girl from Israel, and she served Naaman's wife. She said to her mistress, "If only my master would see the prophet who is in Samaria! He would cure him of his leprosy."

Naaman went to his master and told him what the girl from Israel had said. "By all means, go," the king of Aram replied. "I will send a letter to the king of Israel." So Naaman left, taking with him ten talents of silver, six thousand shekels of gold and ten sets of clothing. The letter that he took to the king of Israel read: "With this letter I am sending my servant Naaman to you so that you may cure him of his leprosy."

As soon as the king of Israel read the letter, he tore his robes and said, "Am I God? Can I kill and bring back to life? Why does this fellow send someone to me to be cured of his leprosy? See how he is trying to pick a quarrel with me!"

When Elisha the man of God heard that the king of Israel had torn his robes, he sent him this message: "Why have you torn your robes? Have the man come to me and he will know that there is a prophet in Israel." So Naaman went with his horses and chariots and stopped at the door of Elisha's house. Elisha sent a messenger to say to him, "Go, wash yourself seven times in the Jordan, and your flesh will be restored and you will be cleansed."

But Naaman went away angry and said, "I thought that he would surely come out to me and stand and call on the name of the Lord his God, wave his hand over the spot and cure me of my leprosy. Are not Abana and Pharpar, the rivers of Damascus, better than all the waters of Israel? Couldn't I wash in them and be cleansed?" So he turned and went off in a rage.

Naaman's servants went to him and said, "My father, if the prophet had told you to do some great thing, would you not have done it? How much more, then, when he tells you, 'Wash and be cleansed'!" So he went down and dipped himself in the Jordan seven times, as the man of God had told him, and his flesh was restored and became clean like that of a young boy.

2 Kings 5:1-14

Seek the peace and prosperity of the city to which I have carried you into exile. Pray to the Lord for it, because if it prospers, you too will prosper.

Jeremiah 29:7

How do you react when wrong things happen? Are you indignant, angry or keen to see justice done? What if you heard that young girls were being kidnapped from their homes and made to work as slaves in another country? You may be outraged and ready to make a generous donation to whatever charity is working to prevent such injustice.

The story of Naaman shows us that the counterintuitive choice to repay evil with good can have far-reaching implications. God honored a young girl's faith with an amazing miracle that changed her master not only physically, but spiritually.

We are so quick to feel like the victims of our circumstances. Consider this young girl's story. Naaman was the commander of the army of Aram; he led raids against the Israelites, carried off their women and children and destroyed their homes. On one such raid, he brought back a young girl as a slave and maidservant to his wife. This young girl was taken from all that she knew to a strange land and an unfamiliar culture. She was blessed in that she was placed with a wealthy family, but she would have watched helplessly as Naaman repeatedly left home to raid her homeland and imprison her people.

Naaman's leprosy may have meant that his family faced financial disaster and social exclusion once the news spread. This was just the disaster most of us would feel he deserved, had he taken us captive in a foreign country. Yet this young girl honored her master; she chose to tell his wife stories of a prophet from Israel who could restore him by the power of God.

This choice was nothing short of outrageous given her circumstances. Most of us probably would have served Naaman's wife begrudgingly at best, but with Israel in the dust and herself a slave in another country, this young servant girl somehow looked past her tragic story and saw a bigger picture. She embraced the opportunity to bless her captor, and he was rewarded with healing.

The young girl in this story is not named; all we know about her is that her heart sought to bless the family she was forced to serve. There must have been something different in her eyes because we know that her mistress listened to her and trusted her.

When bad things happen to us, we are apt to blame God or others. We rarely look for the possibilities God has given us within seemingly unfortunate circumstances. If we remember who we really are, a few simple words spoken at the right time can change the course of a life. Instead of being overcome by evil, we can overcome evil with good (Romans 12:21). *Lord, help me to see the possibilities God has given me in the next few days!*

In what way, if any, do you feel trapped by circumstances? Has God put you close to people He wants to bless through you?

Making Right Choices in Times of Crisis

Then Haman said to King Xerxes, "There is a certain people dispersed and scattered among the peoples in all the provinces of your kingdom who keep themselves separate. Their customs are different from those of all other people, and they do not obey the king's laws; it is not in the king's best interest to tolerate them. If it pleases the king, let a decree be issued to destroy them, and I will give ten thousand talents of silver to the king's administrators for the royal treasury."

So the king took his signet ring from his finger and gave it to Haman son of Hammedatha, the Agagite, the enemy of the Jews. "Keep the money," the king said to Haman, "and do with the people as you please."

Then on the thirteenth day of the first month the royal secretaries were summoned. They wrote out in the script of each province and in the language of each people all Haman's orders to the king's satraps, the governors of the various provinces and the nobles of the various peoples. These were written in the name of King Xerxes himself and sealed with his own ring. Dispatches were sent by couriers to all the king's provinces with the order to destroy, kill and annihilate all the Jews — young and old, women and little children — on a single day, the thirteenth day of the twelfth month, the month of Adar, and to plunder their goods. A copy of the text of the edict was to be issued as law in every province and made known to the people of every nationality so they would be ready for that day.

The couriers went out, spurred on by the king's command and the edict was issued in the citadel of Susa. The king and Haman sat down to drink, but the city of Susa was bewildered.

When Mordecai learned of all that had been done, he tore his clothes, put on sackcloth and ashes, and went out into the city, wailing loudly and bitterly. But he went only as far as the king's gate, because no one clothed in sackcloth was allowed to enter it. In every province to which the edict and order of the king came, there was great mourning among the Jews, with fasting, weeping and wailing. Many lay in sackcloth and ashes.

When Esther's maids and eunuchs came and told her about Mordecai, she was in great distress. She sent clothes for him to put on instead of his sackcloth, but he would not accept them. Then Esther summoned Hathach, one of the king's eunuchs assigned to attend her, and ordered him to find out what was troubling Mordecai and why.

So Hathach went out to Mordecai in the open square of the city in front of the king's gate. Mordecai told him everything that had happened to him, including the exact amount of money Haman had promised to pay into the royal treasury for the destruction of the Jews. He also gave him a copy of the text of the edict for their annihilation, which had been published in Susa, to show to Esther and explain it to her, and he told him to urge her to go into the king's presence to beg for mercy and plead with him for her people.

Hathach went back and reported to Esther what Mordecai had said. Then she instructed him to say to Mordecai, "All the king's officials and the people of the royal provinces know that for any man or woman who approaches the king in the inner court without being summoned the king has but one law: that he be put to death. The only exception to this is for the king to extend the gold scepter to him and spare his life. But thirty days have passed since I was called to go to the king."

When Esther's words were reported to Mordecai, he sent back this answer:

"Do not think that because you are in the king's house you alone of all the Jews will escape. For if you remain silent at this time, relief and deliverance for the Jews will arise from another place, but you and your father's family will perish. And who knows but that you have come to your royal position for such a time as this?"

Then Esther sent this reply to Mordecai: "Go, gather together all the Jews who are in Susa, and fast for me. Do not eat or drink for three days, night or day. I and my attendants will fast as you do. When this is done, I will go to the king, even though it is against the law. And if I perish, I perish."

Esther 3:8 - 4:16 (NIV)

Who wouldn't jump at the chance to win a million dollars? Wealth and success are some of today's most coveted prizes. Many seek to "get rich quick" without real effort. It's easy to expect wealth to be as readily available as everything else in our culture, yet there is rarely such a thing as overnight success. When you look at the stories of most successful people, you'll see that years of preparation precede their achievements or moment of success

Esther's opportunity to speak to the king on behalf of her nation came after years of faithful, godly living. She had spent her life becoming a gentle, trusting and submissive woman. Countless times, she had allowed God to shape her character by trusting Him within her circumstances. She hadn't allowed her beauty to go to her head or her influential position to affect her character.

Who wouldn't want to be such a woman of God? But are we prepared to pay the price each day and allow God to shape us into such women?

The Bible doesn't tell us about Esther's childhood or how she handled the tragic loss of her parents. We don't read about the small decisions she made or her hardworking attitude. But we do see that she chose to submit to her cousin and adopted father, Mordecai, daily, and we are privileged to catch a glimpse of the moment in her life when she made an incredibly courageous choice. She chose to do what was right for her nation rather than worry about her own life.

Esther became a woman who "won the favor of everyone who saw her." We read that King Xerxes chose her to be his wife from among many other girls because of her astonishing beauty. Experience tells us that beauty is no guarantee of good character, and we know that it takes a person of great character to wear beauty graciously.

Esther acted wisely and patiently in the face of a very distressing problem. She had no job description for her position as queen, and there was no path clearly laid out for her to follow. Instead, she relied on prayer and Mordecai's advice.

When Mordecai asked her to speak with Xerxes, it would have been all too easy to succumb to self-doubt or pride. The king hadn't called for her in thirty days, and she could have chosen to question his love for her, focusing on insecurity instead of the truth that she was a chosen woman and beloved of God.

The king could have had her killed for daring to enter his presence uninvited. It would have been so easy for her to succumb to fear, but Esther threw a great banquet for the king and showed amazing humility as she spoke with him afterwards. She told him that she wouldn't have usually troubled him and explained that she had only disturbed him because her people faced annihilation. Esther exhibited great wisdom in the plan she proposed to King Xerxes, which allowed him to save her people by superseding the decree he had already issued without losing face.

Years of faithfully making conscious choices for God had prepared Esther for this moment. Her character was formed, her mind was made up and her path was clear. Her brave decision saved a nation.

God wants us to allow Him to shape our characters and our future, trusting and submitting to His plan and purpose.

What has God called you to do in this hostile world?

What is God teaching you at this moment? Are you submitting to Him or resisting His moulding of your character?

Holding on to the Promises of God

There was also a prophet, Anna, the daughter of Penuel, of the tribe of Asher. She was very old; she had lived with her husband seven years after her marriage, and then was a widow until she was eighty-four. She never left the temple but worshiped night and day, fasting and praying. Coming up to them at that very moment, she gave thanks to God and spoke about the child to all who were looking forward to the redemption of Jerusalem.

Luke 2:36-38

If God called you to be the lowest of the low, how would you respond? Would you be happy to be a street beggar in the slums of India? What about an AIDS victim suffering in Africa?

If we're honest, we are usually able to handle the lows in our lives because we know that we have positive things to look forward to. What if there was no guaranteed comfort, no basis for hope in a better future? Most of us would probably struggle to trust God in such a situation.

In his brief account of Anna, Luke told of a woman whose hopes of a long, happy family life were dashed when her husband died after only seven years of marriage. She was left to live alone as a widow for over sixty years, totally dependent on others for every daily need, possibly even the roof over her head. At some point, Anna decided to choose trust over bitterness, faith over anger and hope over despair. In her old age, she continued to focus on the things of God and served Him at the temple. She chose to trust God's promises, believing and praying them back to God.

Facing heartbreak after losing her husband in her early twenties, it would have been easy for Anna to wallow in self-pity, easy to be angry at the unfortunate turn her life had taken. All her hopes and dreams — including motherhood — were in ruins, and she knew that she was condemned to many years of living as a penniless widow, the lowest of the low in Jewish society.

We read that Anna dedicated her life to waiting and hoping for the promised Messiah, praying and fasting for God's kingdom to come. She showed incredible patience and perseverance as she spent every day in the temple for over sixty years. She still expected God to break into her world, even after so many years with no sign of the Messiah. But Anna knew God's Word and kept on asking Him to fulfill His promises and send the Messiah.

In her old age, we see that she found and fulfilled her role in God's kingdom, in which there is no retirement age. Anna's reward for such devotion was, incredibly, that she got to see the young face of Jesus Christ, the promised Messiah. When Mary and Joseph brought Him to the temple, as was the custom, God revealed to Anna that this young boy was the long-awaited Messiah.

Whilst it can be difficult to hold on to God's promises through difficult circumstances, we see that Anna allowed God to use them positively in her life. She trusted Him to send the Messiah and was gloriously rewarded for her years of patience and prayer.

What does God promise you in His Word?

Can you choose to trust Him within your circumstances?

Ask Him to give you faith to believe His promises in your life.

God's Grace for the Fallen Sinner

Joshua said to the two men who had spied out the land, "Go into the prostitute's house and bring her out and all who belong to her, in accordance with your oath to her." So the young men who had done the spying went in and brought out Rahab, her father and mother, her brothers and sisters and all who belonged to her. They brought out her entire family and put them in a place outside the camp of Israel.

Then they burned the whole city and everything in it, but they put the silver and gold and the articles of bronze and iron into the treasury of the Lords house. But Joshua spared Rahab the prostitute, with her family and all who belonged to her, because she hid the men Joshua had sent as spies to Jericho—and she lives among the Israelites to this day.

Joshua 6:22-25

You can read the full story in Joshua 2.

Do you ever look on people and think they're too far gone for God to save them? Perhaps their sins seem too great, or their lives too broken. If we're honest, most of us have probably thought this about someone at some point. Whether it's because they've gone off the rails, are too proud, too hurt or just too far from God and deep in sin, most of us struggle to believe that God can touch and rescue family, friends and colleagues we know.

The story of Rahab demonstrates that no one is too deeply rooted in sin to receive God's grace. We see that there is nothing God will not do to restore the lost, no lengths to which He will not go to save just one person. Whatever labels society puts on someone, God sees them differently and has good plans for their life.

Rahab was a prostitute in the city of Jericho. We don't know how or why she came to choose this profession. Everyone in Jericho had probably heard the same stories about the Israelite army approaching the city. They had heard about how God dried up the Red Sea and how the Israelites had utterly destroyed two Amorite kingdoms. But of all the people in that city, Rahab alone placed her faith in the God of Israel. She saw what was going to happen and who it was that was in control of events. "I know that the Lord has given you this land... for the Lord your God is God in heaven above and on the earth below," she said.

Rahab took action. She offered lodging to the spies who were sent to scope out the city. When the king of Jericho asked her to hand over the spies, she courageously defied him, saying that they had already left, when, in fact, they were still hiding out on her roof. Because

Rahab risked her own life for strangers, the Israelite spies promised to spare her and her family when the city fell.

When the walls of Jericho crumbled, Rahab and her family were the only ones spared from the destruction of the city and its inhabitants. She and her family reaped a great reward for her faith in Israel's God.

Later we read that Rahab became the bride of an Israelite and bore a son, whom she named Boaz. The woman who was once an outsider was grafted right into the family of God. Incredibly, Matthew 1:5 even lists her name in the genealogy of Jesus Christ, among many other sinners who may seem utterly unfit to precede such a King unless you understand God's love for the lost and outcast.

The Bible tells us that "God is not willing that any should perish" (2 Peter 3:9). If you're outraged that Rahab is included in the genealogy of Christ, how much more so that we sinners, as part of His church, should be called the bride of Christ?

Rahab is mentioned eight times in the Bible. Five of those eight times, she is called "Rahab the prostitute." Does God seek to remind us of her shameful sin? Surely not. God loves to display His grace in the lives of restored sinners. He longs to turn each of our lives into expressions of His immense grace and boundless love. God showed His delight in rescuing and restoring the lost by taking Rahab from nowhere and bringing her right into the heart of His family.

Without His grace and Christ's death and resurrection, you would be lost and without hope. Take a few moments to thank God for His grace to you as a Christ-follower.

Jesus Knows Our Shame

Now he had to go through Samaria. So he came to a town in Samaria called Sychar, near the plot of ground Jacob had given to his son Joseph. Jacob's well was there, and Jesus, tired as he was from the journey, sat down by the well. It was about noon.

When a Samaritan woman came to draw water, Jesus said to her, "Will you give me a drink?" (His disciples had gone into the town to buy food.)

The Samaritan woman said to him, "You are a Jew and I am a Samaritan woman. How can you ask me for a drink?" (For Jews do not associate with Samaritans.[a])

Jesus answered her, "If you knew the gift of God and who it is that asks you for a drink, you would have asked him and he would have given you living water."

"Sir," the woman said, "you have nothing to draw with and the well is deep. Where can you get this living water? Are you greater than our father Jacob, who gave us the well and drank from it himself, as did also his sons and his livestock?"

Jesus answered, "Everyone who drinks this water will be thirsty again, but whoever drinks the water I give them will never thirst. Indeed, the water I give them will become in them a spring of water welling up to eternal life."

The woman said to him, "Sir, give me this water so that I won't get thirsty and have to keep coming here to draw water."

He told her, "Go, call your husband and come back."

"I have no husband," she replied.

Jesus said to her, "You are right when you say you have no husband. The fact is, you have had five husbands, and the man you now have is not your husband. What you have just said is quite true

...

Then, leaving her water jar, the woman went back to the town and said to the people, "Come, see a man who told me everything I ever did. Could this be the Messiah?"

John 4:4-18 & 28:29

You can read the full story in John 4:1-42.

Don't you hate it when people make snap judgments about you?
Have you ever had someone judge you based only on your appearance? Maybe they've judged your accent, the size of your house or the make of your car. It can be annoying and even infuriating when others base our intrinsic worth on such inconsequential things.

Yet how would you react if a scantily dressed, heavily made-up, tattooed woman showed up at your church? What about a woman who had a reputation for immoral living? Honestly? Most of us would probably struggle to get past our judgmental old natures before approaching, talking with and befriending her. Many of us make snap judgements based on appearance or our past experience.

The Samaritan woman at the well was such a woman. She was viewed with scorn and derision for the immoral life she lived, yet Jesus crossed cultural divides, social norms and pre-conceived notions to speak with her. Why? He wants us to understand that there is nothing we can do to escape the bounds of His love, nowhere we can go where His love doesn't reach out to us. No sin is too great for Him to forgive. No shame is too far for Him to reach out to us. He wants us to know that we are loved and accepted just as we are.

Don't let familiarity with this Bible story cause you to miss the love of Christ or how far Jesus is willing to go to reach one lost woman. To Him, every individual is exceedingly important.

To fully appreciate this passage, it's helpful to understand how Jews traditionally viewed Samaritans. Imagine how a relative of a 9/11 victim might feel about the terrorists who perpetrated the atrocity.

That's how Jews felt about Samaritans. Talking to someone from that culture and belief system would probably be very emotionally difficult, let alone sharing a drink together. Yet Jesus — who was a Jew through and through — not only chose to associate Himself with the Samaritan woman, He engaged in conversation with her. His actions were rather simply outrageous for a Jew at that time.

Who was this woman and what was her story? In a land that got very hot during the middle of the day, the people traditionally collected water in the early morning or during the evening. Women would often go to the well in groups for safety and to enjoy each other's company. The fact that the Samaritan woman was visiting the well alone in the heat of the day says much about her position in society.

She may have been shunned by the respectable women who looked down on her. She lived with the shame of having five ex-husbands and was living with a man who was not her husband. Shame was her identity, and it's all her neighbors saw when they passed her in the street.

Jesus not only approached her; He accepted her even before He mentioned the sin that they were both so aware of. Isn't that awesome? He accepted her first, and only then did He confront her sin.

The result? She was forgiven — once again able to hold her head high because her shame was instantly gone. She was so amazed by Jesus that she told everyone about Him. The woman who avoided society by going to the well in the heat of the day was transformed. She immediately became an evangelist to her village, and as a result, many lives were touched and changed by Jesus.

How will you respond to Jesus, now that you know that He loves and accepts you in spite of your shame?

Are there feelings of shame that you can bring to Him and receive His loving forgiveness and healing touch today?

Waiting for God's Timing

Now Laban had two daughters; the name of the older was Leah, and the name of the younger was Rachel. Leah had weak eyes, but Rachel had a lovely figure and was beautiful. Jacob was in love with Rachel and said, "I'll work for you seven years in return for your younger daughter Rachel."

Laban said, "It's better that I give her to you than to some other man. Stay here with me." So Jacob served seven years to get Rachel, but they seemed like only a few days to him because of his love for her

....

God remembered Rachel; he listened to her and enabled her to conceive. She became pregnant and gave birth to a son and said, "God has taken away my disgrace." She named him Joseph.

Genesis 30:16-20 & 22-24

The Lord is not slow in keeping his promise, as some understand slowness. He is patient with you, not wanting anyone to perish, but everyone to come to repentance.

2 Peter 3:9

You can read the full story in Genesis 29:1-31:55; 35:16-30.

Do you love watching a good romantic movie? There's something uplifting and encouraging about a good dose of romance.

The story of Rachel may seem romantic at first glance. We read of how Jacob instantly fell deeply in love with her and agreed to work seven years to win her as his wife. Yet, if we dig a little deeper, we find a flawed woman just like us. Rachel was prone to foolish decisions, impatience, even lies and jealousy. Even though she had much that we might desire, God had much to teach her.

After her father tricked Jacob into marrying her older sister, Leah, the beautiful Rachel finally became his second wife. She was the woman Jacob loved, and after he worked seven years to win her hand, she could not have doubted his love.

But after they were married, Rachel had to endure the social stigma and embarrassment of infertility. In Jewish culture, being childless was seen as a punishment from God. Rachel watched as her sister bore six children to Jacob, and then her maidservant, Bilhah, and Leah's maidservant, Zilpah, both had children fathered by Jacob. Rachel remained barren.

At one point, Rachel was so jealous in her despair that she cried to Jacob, "Give me children, or I'll die!" He responded in anger, saying, "Am I in the place of God, who has kept you from having children?"(Genesis 30:1-2)

Poor Rachel was beautiful and loved, but she had to endure years of shame and humiliation. Eventually she realized that she should ask God for her miracle baby. We read that "God remembered Rachel; he listened to her and opened her womb." (Genesis 30:22) This account doesn't tell us that Rachel was forgotten by God; rather, He faithfully answered her prayer when it was time for Him to act on His promise. Finally Rachel bore a child — a son — Joseph, a child with an incredible destiny.

Rachel had Jacob's love, but wanted his children. Leah had his children, but longed for his love. Doesn't this ring true today, that we aren't always thankful for what we have? We tend to look at others and desire what they have instead of being thankful for what we have already.

In our world of instant everything, one of our greatest temptations is to expect our wants to be satisfied immediately. Once we have the big, widescreen TV, we tend to desire our next acquisition. We may buy one designer outfit or an expensive gadget, only to find ourselves longing for another new toy. We can end up continually striving for more.

Rachel's story depicts the importance of waiting for God's perfect timing. Her son Joseph was destined to become an influential leader in Egypt who would save his people from famine. God had a far bigger plan for her and her son than Rachel could ever have imagined.

God is masterfully weaving the detailed tapestry of human history. He wants your story to be beautifully woven in. Will you wait patiently for all that you are hoping and longing for and allow Him to weave His pattern perfectly in your life?

In what way are you waiting for God to fulfill His promises? Are you regularly praying for Him to bring them to fulfillment? Ask God to teach you patience as you wait to see His promises fulfilled.

The Truth Will Overcome Your Accusers

Judah got a wife for Er, his firstborn, and her name was Tamar. But Er, Judah's firstborn, was wicked in the Lord's sight; so the Lord put him to death.

Then Judah said to Onan, "Sleep with your brother's wife and fulfill your duty to her as a brother-in-law to raise up offspring for your brother." But Onan knew that the child would not be his; so whenever he slept with his brother's wife, he spilled his semen on the ground to keep from providing offspring for his brother. What he did was wicked in the Lord's sight; so the Lord put him to death also.

Judah then said to his daughter-in-law Tamar, "Live as a widow in your father's household until my son Shelah grows up." For he thought, "He may die too, just like his brothers." So Tamar went to live in her father's household.

After a long time Judah's wife, the daughter of Shua, died. When Judah had recovered from his grief, he went up to Timnah, to the men who were shearing his sheep, and his friend Hirah the Adullamite went with him.

When Tamar was told, "Your father-in-law is on his way to Timnah to shear his sheep," she took off her widow's clothes, covered herself with a veil to disguise herself, and then sat down at the entrance to Enaim, which is on the road to Timnah. For she saw that, though Shelah had now grown up, she had not been given to him as his wife.

When Judah saw her, he thought she was a prostitute, for she had covered her face. Not realizing that she was his daughter-in-law, he went over to her by the roadside and said, "Come now, let me sleep with you."

"And what will you give me to sleep with you?" she asked.

"I'll send you a young goat from my flock," he said.

"Will you give me something as a pledge until you send it?" she asked.

He said, "What pledge should I give you?"

"Your seal and its cord, and the staff in your hand," she answered. So he gave them to her and slept with her, and she became pregnant by him. After she left, she took off her veil and put on her widow's clothes again.

Meanwhile Judah sent the young goat by his friend the Adullamite in order to get his pledge back from the woman, but he did not find her. He asked the men who lived there, "Where is the shrine prostitute who was beside the road at Enaim?"

"There hasn't been any shrine prostitute here," they said.

So he went back to Judah and said, "I didn't find her. Besides, the men who lived there said, 'There hasn't been any shrine prostitute here.'"

Then Judah said, "Let her keep what she has, or we will become a laughingstock. After all, I did send her this young goat, but you didn't find her."

About three months later Judah was told, "Your daughter-in-law Tamar is guilty of prostitution, and as a result she is now pregnant."

Judah said, "Bring her out and have her burned to death!"

As she was being brought out, she sent a message to her father-in-law. "I am pregnant by the man who owns these," she said. And she added, "See if you recognize whose seal and cord and staff these are."

Judah recognized them and said, "She is more righteous than I, since I wouldn't give her to my son Shelah." And he did not sleep with her again.

Genesis 38:6-26

Do not be overcome by evil, but overcome evil with good.

Romans 12:21

Don't you hate it when you know that people are whispering about you behind your back? It is difficult to know how to respond and sometimes hard not to retaliate. It's especially painful when they are wrong about you or, worse still, when they are intentionally spreading lies.

Tamar faced whispers and lies from her mother-in-law when not one, but two of her wicked husbands died at God's hand. Can you imagine the whispers that went around the village about her? The fear in children's eyes as this woman who was 'responsible' for the death of two husbands (Genesis 38:6-10) passed by on the street? What a reputation for any woman to live with.

But the way Tamar handled her situation shows us that however unfair circumstances seem and no matter how high the odds are stacked against us, there is a way for us to honor God in the midst of trouble. If we cling to the truth and act righteously, with God's help we will eventually overcome evil.

As a childless widow, Tamar was the lowest of the low in her society. Although it was her right to marry Judah's youngest son, anger and fear prevented her father-in-law from doing what was right according to the law. His lack of action would have brought shame upon himself, Tamar and his family.

As the realization of this impending shame dawned on Tamar, she made a bold choice that was within her legal rights. She disguised herself as a roadside prostitute and, with her face covered, slept with Judah. She conceived a child as a result.

When her pregnancy was discovered, Tamar faced being burned to death because she had no husband. Yet she was wise: She had obtained a pledge from Judah — his seal, cord and staff. She produced these and sent them to him as an answer to her accusers. When Judah realized the truth of what had happened, he said of Tamar, "She is more righteous than I" (Genesis 38:26) because he knew that she had saved his family from shame.

When we are accused or misunderstood, a natural response is to confront our accusers, yet Tamar's shows us another way of responding to our accusers. She waited patiently to see if her father-in-law would come through in obedience and give her in marriage to his youngest son. When it became clear that this was not a part of Judah's plan, she put her plan into action.

While her actions may seem abhorrent to us, the Bible tells us that Tamar was a godly woman who acted in accordance with the law. Her actions in obtaining what was rightfully hers not only brought her the honor she was due, they also saved her father-in-law and freed him from his own shame. Her actions secured the family line which may otherwise have died out.

Tamar didn't blame the social system or Judah's lack of action. She didn't sink to the level of her accusers or become embroiled in arguments or accusations. Instead, she acted courageously to make things right. She didn't take the law into her own hands. As a result, she and her twin sons earned a place in the lineage of Christ (Matthew 1:3) and are proudly mentioned in the book of Ruth (Ruth 4:12).

When we are faced with unfair accusations and lies, there is one sure way to protect our hearts. Trusting and patiently following the Word of God is a tried and tested way to keep us safe until, in time, we are vindicated and the truth comes to light.

Is God speaking to you about how you can handle those who falsely accuse you or speak unkindly about you?

Time to Get Moving

Then he prayed "Lord, God of my master Abraham, make me successful today, and show kindness to my master Abraham. See, I am standing beside this spring, and the daughters of the townspeople are coming out to draw water. May it be that when I say to a young woman, 'Please let down your jar that I may have a drink,' and she says, 'Drink, and I'll water your camels too'—let her be the one you have chosen for your servant Isaac. By this I will know that you have shown kindness to my master."

Before he had finished praying, Rebekah came out with her jar on her shoulder. She was the daughter of Bethuel son of Milkah, who was the wife of Abraham's brother Nahor. The woman was very beautiful, a virgin; no man had ever slept with her. She went down to the spring, filled her jar and came up again.

The servant hurried to meet her and said, "Please give me a little water from your jar."

Drink, my lord," she said, and quickly lowered the jar to her hands and gave him a drink.

After she had given him a drink, she said, "I'll draw water for your camels too, until they have had enough to drink." So she quickly emptied her jar into the trough, ran back to the well to draw more water, and drew enough for all his camels. Without saying a word, the man watched her closely to learn whether or not the Lord had made his journey successful.

When the camels had finished drinking, the man took out a gold nose ring weighing a beka and two gold bracelets weighing ten shekels. Then he asked, "Whose daughter are you? Please tell me, is there room in your father's house for us to spend the night?"

She answered him, "I am the daughter of Bethuel, the son that Milkah bore to Nahor." And she added, "We have plenty of straw and fodder, as well as room for you to spend the night."

Then the man bowed down and worshiped the Lord, saying, "Praise be to the Lord, the God of my master Abraham, who has not abandoned his kindness and faithfulness to my master. As for me, the Lord has led me on the journey to the house of my master's relatives."

Genesis 24:12-27

Be still before the Lord and wait patiently for himmy master's relatives."

Psalm 37:7

You can read the full story in Genesis 24; 25:19-26; 27:1-17.

How patiently are you prepared to wait for the fulfillment of your dreams? Would you wait for a day, a month or a year? Would thirty years seem too long before all that you long for finally happens?

Like many young girls, Rebekah dreamt of getting married and having children, but she didn't sit at home talking about it with friends, wringing her hands and wondering if she would ever marry. She kept busy serving her family, helping out with household chores such as drawing water from the well. In doing so, she was perfectly positioned for God's plans and purposes for her life.

Sometimes we're so busy waiting for God to answer our prayers that we sit waiting for an answer instead of living faithful, purposeful lives in the meantime. When our hearts are fixed on God, we may find ourselves pleasantly surprised by what "just happens" in our lives.

Abraham wanted to choose a wife for his son, Isaac. He did not want a Canaanite woman, though he was living among Canaanites; he wanted to choose from among his own people. So Abraham sent his servant with clear instructions to find an honorable wife from the family and home he had left behind in his native land.

The servant sat by the spring and asked God to show him which woman he should choose for Isaac. He prepared some questions to ask the women, to see if they were of good character. Rebekah was the first woman to arrive. Abraham's servant asked her to draw him some water, which she did, and then she offered to draw water for his camels. The servant then learned that Rebekah was the grand-daughter of Abraham's brother — she met every requirement.

Sometimes we're so busy longing for God to do something that we lapse into inactivity waiting for Him, but God loves to involve us in working out His purposes. As we step out in faith, He shapes our characters and makes us more like Jesus. Have you heard the phrase, "You can't steer a ship that's not moving"? Our answer may be simply to get moving, confident that God is faithful to guide us.

Rebekah didn't sit and wait until Abraham's servant came to the spring. Over years of patience, she learned to submit to her parents and to serve others humbly and happily. She allowed God to mould her character, shaping her into a godly woman with a pure heart.

The same is true for us. If you believe that God has a good plan for your life, what are you doing today to prepare yourself? Are you showing yourself faithful in the small things (Luke 16:10)? Are you serving others? Are you spending your time productively? Are you developing and practicing your gifts?

As you step out, be prepared for God to meet you in your journey.

How are you allowing God to shape your character as you wait expectantly for His promises to be fulfilled? Are you stepping out and believing what God has promised you?

What is your next step?

Wealthy, Influential and Totally Sold-Out for Jesus

After this, Jesus traveled about from one town and village to another, proclaiming the good news of the kingdom of God. The Twelve were with him, and also some women who had been cured of evil spirits and diseases: Mary (called Magdalene) from whom seven demons had come out; Joanna the wife of Chuza, the manager of Herod's household; Susanna; and many others. These women were helping to support them out of their own means.

Luke 8:1-3

You can also read about Joanna in Luke 24:1-12.

Ever dream of winning millions? What would you do if you won a fortune? What would you spend it on, and who would you share it with? What lifestyle might you live? Do you picture yourself as a celebrity in a shimmering dress, being photographed by the paparazzi as you sway down the red carpet?

When Herod was king, Joanna was somewhat of a celebrity. Her husband, Chuza, was a man of influence who managed Herod's household. This couple would have been invited to parties with the famous and wealthy of their time.

Luke tells us that Joanna was one of a number of women following Jesus who had been "cured of evil spirits and diseases." As a wealthy woman, she would have been able to afford the best doctors and physicians who, despite all their efforts, had been unable to cure her. Then Jesus came and her encounter with him changed her life completely in a moment.

Joanna's response was to give back. She gave generously, and her giving cost her. She was fully aware of the risks that came with following Jesus, but she wanted nothing more than to serve and be with Him.

Because of Chuza's prominent position and wealth, there were expectations regarding how he and Joanna should live. Herod's lifestyle was well-known, and he certainly wasn't to be challenged. This was the man who would ultimately order the murder of John the Baptist. His father had tried to kill Jesus when he was a baby by ordering the slaughter of all male newborns in Bethlehem.

Following Jesus was not an easy option, and going public was risky for both Joanna and her husband. It could have led to rumors about her loyalty, upset the king and even run the risk of death. It took a brave but secure woman to walk this path, and Joanna made such a choice. Jesus had changed her life, and she lovingly gave Him everything in return.

In order for the kingdom of God to advance, God needs people who will give freely. Joanna was one in the crowd that followed Jesus; she gave from her own resources to support His ministry. He still needs people who will evaluate their own lifestyles and make costly choices in order to give generously.

Joanna was among the women who saw the empty tomb after Jesus' resurrection. What an incredible privilege to see the risen Christ! As we follow Jesus, we cannot know where He will lead us. Joanna was a committed follower, willing to count the costs in her life; she was totally sold-out for Jesus. Her humble response to His unconditional love brought her joy and set her free to love, live and give extravagantly.

What is your response to Jesus' life-changing love today?

Is God calling you to live and give more extravagantly?

Transforming Power

When one of the Pharisees invited Jesus to have dinner with him, he went to the Pharisee's house and reclined at the table. A woman in that town who lived a sinful life learned that Jesus was eating at the Pharisee's house, so she came there with an alabaster jar of perfume. As she stood behind him at his feet weeping, she began to wet his feet with her tears. Then she wiped them with her hair, kissed them and poured perfume on them.

When the Pharisee who had invited him saw this, he said to himself, "If this man were a prophet, he would know who is touching him and what kind of woman she is—that she is a sinner."

Jesus answered him, "Simon, I have something to tell you."

"Tell me, teacher," he said.

"Two people owed money to a certain moneylender. One owed him five hundred denarii, and the other fifty. Neither of them had the money to pay him back, so he forgave the debts of both. Now which of them will love him more?"

Simon replied, "I suppose the one who had the bigger debt forgiven."

"You have judged correctly," Jesus said.

Then he turned toward the woman and said to Simon, "Do you see this woman? I came into your house. You did not give me any water for my feet, but she wet my feet with her tears and wiped them with her hair. You did not give me a kiss, but this woman, from the time I entered, has not stopped kissing my feet. You did not put oil on my head, but she has poured perfume on my feet. Therefore, I tell you, her many sins have been forgiven—as her great love has shown. But whoever has been forgiven little loves little."

Then Jesus said to her, "Your sins are forgiven."

The other guests began to say among themselves, "Who is this who even forgives sins?"

Jesus said to the woman, "Your faith has saved you; go in peace.

Luke 7:36-50

When did you last look deep into the eyes of a loved one? Have you experienced the feeling of being the only two people in the room, though you were in the midst of a crowd? Can you remember ever feeling totally loved and accepted by someone, even just for a moment? If so, you can probably remember who and where it was.

Luke tells the story of a sinful woman with a damaged reputation, someone not welcomed in society, who finally discovered love and acceptance she had been seeking.

As Jesus shared a meal with a Pharisee named Simon and his friends (a bunch of religious men who had clear guidelines and strict rules about what was right and proper), a woman interrupted their conversation with her weeping. It was certainly not acceptable for any woman to disturb their meal, let alone the woman they view as the most sinful woman in town.

She knew what Simon was like, how frosty his response to her would be. She may have been fearful, wondering what people would say, but still she entered Simon's house. There was something different about Jesus, and she had to go to Him.

As she approached Jesus, so aware of her sin, she was overcome with emotion and began to weep in His presence. Incredibly, in this room full of wealthy and important men, Jesus turned to face her.

Just imagine that sweet moment with Jesus.

Amidst many so-called "holy" men, Jesus turned toward one woman and for that moment, it was just the two of them. She looked into the eyes of Jesus, the Son of God, and saw only love and acceptance.

Jesus forgave her many sins and told her to "go in peace." She who knew no peace for such a long time was restored and forgiven.

Jesus wants to use this beautiful account to teach us an important lesson about forgiveness. It's easy to become distracted by our busy lives. As we interact with imperfect people, judgmental thoughts tempt us, and we may find ourselves criticizing them and muttering behind their backs. We could probably even justify ourselves, even though it's just a symptom of our own pride.

This woman came to Jesus and anointed His feet. She washed them with her tears and dried them with her hair, and in so doing she showed us that He is all that really matters. While distractions are many, we need to push past them to make our way to Jesus' feet. Everything in your life boils down to you and Jesus. We need to push through the distractions and humbly come to Him.

As we acknowledge our sin and come to give rather than receive, something wonderful happens. We find ourselves alone with Jesus, His loving eyes looking deep into ours and declaring that our sins have been forgiven. We can experience His love and acceptance today and every day.

Come quietly to Jesus' feet today and spend some precious moments with Him. He alone can offer you true peace and forgiveness.

Holding Fast Through Life's Storms

There was a certain man from Ramathaim, a Zuphite from the hill country of Ephraim, whose name was Elkanah son of Jeroham, the son of Elihu, the son of Tohu, the son of Zuph, an Ephraimite. He had two wives; one was called Hannah and the other Peninnah. Peninnah had children, but Hannah had none.

Year after year this man went up from his town to worship and sacrifice to the Lord Almighty at Shiloh, where Hophni and Phinehas, the two sons of Eli, were priests of the Lord. Whenever the day came for Elkanah to sacrifice, he would give portions of the meat to his wife Peninnah and to all her sons and daughters. But to Hannah he gave a double portion because he loved her, and the Lord had closed her womb. Because the Lord had closed Hannah's womb, her rival kept provoking her in order to irritate her. This went on year after year. Whenever Hannah went up to the house of the Lord, her rival provoked her till she wept and would not eat. Her husband Elkanah would say to her, "Hannah, why are you weeping? Why don't you eat? Why are you downhearted? Don't I mean more to you than ten sons?"

Once when they had finished eating and drinking in Shiloh, Hannah stood up. Now Eli the priest was sitting on his chair by the doorpost of the Lord's house. In her deep anguish Hannah prayed to the Lord, weeping bitterly. And she made a vow, saying, "Lord Almighty, if you will only look on your servant's misery and remember me, and not forget your servant but give her a son, then I will give him to the Lord for all the days of his life, and no razor will ever be used on his head."

As she kept on praying to the Lord, Eli observed her mouth. Hannah was praying in her heart, and her lips were moving but her voice was not heard. Eli thought she was drunk and said to her, "How long are you going to stay drunk? Put away your wine."

"Not so, my lord," Hannah replied, "I am a woman who is deeply troubled. I have not been drinking wine or beer; I was pouring out my soul to the Lord. Do not take your servant for a wicked woman; I have been praying here out of my great anguish and grief."

Eli answered, "Go in peace, and may the God of Israel grant you what you have asked of him."

She said, "May your servant find favor in your eyes." Then she went her way and ate something, and her face was no longer downcast.

Early the next morning they arose and worshiped before the Lord and then went back to their home at Ramah. Elkanah made love to his wife Hannah, and the Lord remembered her. So in the course of time Hannah became pregnant and gave birth to a son. She named him Samuel, saying, "Because I asked the Lord for him.""

1 Samuel 1:1-19

And the Lord was gracious to Hannah; she gave birth to three sons and two daughters. Meanwhile, the boy Samuel grew up in the presence of the Lord.

1 Samuel 2:21

How do you respond when you're provoked? Does it depend on how you're feeling at the time? Sometimes our responses are influenced by whether it's a good or bad day or even by our hormones.

Hannah was deeply loved by her husband, but she had never been able to conceive a child. In her Jewish community, this was seen as a disgrace, a judgment from God for hidden sin. Hannah would have felt shame because of her inability to bear children.

To help us relate to the social stigma that Hannah had to live with each day, imagine how you would be received if you were diagnosed with AIDS. How might this change the way your family, friends and co-workers view and respond to you?

Hannah's husband took a second wife, Peninnah, as was permitted by the law. Not only did Peninnah bare many children, but she enjoyed tormenting Hannah and gloating over her. This deeply distressed Hannah, but she remained quiet, humble and self-controlled, despite this provocation.

Amazingly, Hannah did not let her feelings provoke her to anger. Despite years of living with shame and humiliation, she was a model of self-control. That is, until she entered the temple and came before her God. At this point, she poured out the pain in her heart. Silently sobbing her fears, torments and sorrows to the Lord, she expressed her deep desire to have a son.

Even when Eli, the priest, unjustly accuses of being drunk, her response is the model of humility and self control.

Hannah is the model of a godly woman; in an incredibly challenging time, she knew the only One to whom she could bring her heavy burden. She poured her heart out to God and asked Him to do the impossible, to give her a child.

As women, we so often use life's pressures and challenges as excuses. We fly off the handle at those around us, carelessly reacting in anger. We respond to accusations by gossiping about those who treat us unfairly. We may be tempted to compare ourselves to others, and we may even harbor resentment towards God because of our circumstances, rather than bringing our pain before Him — the One who holds all things in His hands.

Hannah's story is meant to challenge us; she showed that it is possible to be provoked and deeply distressed, yet continue to trust in God. Hannah continued to go to the temple, despite the opportunities it gave her rival for more gloating. Hannah knew that God had humbled her for a season, but that He also delights in exalting the needy. She didn't run from God; she clung to Him. And she made a costly promise to give up her firstborn son to serve in the temple as a Nazirite, dedicated to the Lord, if God would answer her prayer.

When God gave her Samuel, in answer to her prayers, Hannah dedicated him to God just as she had promised. Yet God in His goodness did not leave her life empty and childless. She went on to have more sons and daughters — the growing family she waited so long for.

Hannah trusted God to hear her prayers. Even when nothing changed for years, she continued to ask God to intervene and change her life by giving her a child. In a world of instant responses, we have been conditioned to be poor at waiting, yet the kingdom of God is unlike the world. God rewards our patience and persistent prayer. He honors those who patiently bear difficult burdens. He loves the faith of His sons and daughters.

How do you handle the irritations of life?

What is your response when others treat you unjustly?

With tears and prayers, can you take your struggles to Jesus and allow Him to give you the peace and assurance you need?

Whose Team Are You On?

A certain man in Maon, who had property there at Carmel, was very wealthy. He had a thousand goats and three thousand sheep, which he was shearing in Carmel. His name was Nabal and his wife's name was Abigail. She was an intelligent and beautiful woman, but her husband was surly and mean in his dealings — he was a Calebite.

While David was in the wilderness, he heard that Nabal was shearing sheep. So he sent ten young men and said to them, "Go up to Nabal at Carmel and greet him in my name. Say to him: 'Long life to you! Good health to you and your household! And good health to all that is yours!

"'Now I hear that it is sheep-shearing time. When your shepherds were with us, we did not mistreat them, and the whole time they were at Carmel nothing of theirs was missing. Ask your own servants and they will tell you. Therefore be favorable toward my men, since we come at a festive time. Please give your servants and your son David whatever you can find for them.'"

When David's men arrived, they gave Nabal this message in David's name. Then they waited.

Nabal answered David's servants, "Who is this David? Who is this son of Jesse? Many servants are breaking away from their masters these days. Why should I take my bread and water, and the meat I have slaughtered for my shearers, and give it to men coming from who knows where?"

David's men turned around and went back. When they arrived, they reported every word. David said to his men, "Each of you strap on your sword!" So they did, and David strapped his on as well. About four hundred men went up with David, while two hundred stayed with the supplies.

One of the servants told Abigail, Nabal's wife, "David sent messengers from the wilderness to give our master his greetings, but he hurled insults at them. Yet these men were very good to us. They did not mistreat us, and the whole time we were out in the fields near them nothing was missing. Night and day they were a wall around us the whole time we were herding our sheep near them. Now think it over and see what you can do, because disaster is hanging over our master and his whole household. He is such a wicked man that no one can talk to him."

Abigail acted quickly. She took two hundred loaves of bread, two skins of wine, five dressed sheep, five seahs of roasted grain, a hundred cakes of raisins and two hundred cakes of pressed figs, and loaded them on donkeys. Then she told her servants, "Go on ahead; I'll follow you." But she did not tell her husband Nabal.

As she came riding her donkey into a mountain ravine, there were David and his men descending toward her, and she met them. David had just said, "It's been useless — all my watching over this fellow's property in the wilderness so that nothing of his was missing. He has paid me back evil for good. May God deal with David, be it ever so severely, if by morning I leave alive one male of all who belong to him!"

When Abigail saw David, she quickly got off her donkey and bowed down before David with her face to the ground. She fell at his feet and said: "Pardon your servant, my lord, and let me speak to you; hear what your servant has to say. Please pay no attention, my lord, to that wicked man Nabal. He is just like his name—his name means Fool, and folly goes with him. And as for me, your servant, I did not see the men my lord sent. And now, my lord, as surely as the Lord your God lives and as you live, since the Lord has kept you from bloodshed and from avenging yourself with your own hands, may your enemies and all who are intent on harming my lord be like Nabal. And let this gift, which your servant has brought to my lord, be given to the men who follow you.

"Please forgive your servant's presumption. The Lord your God will certainly make a lasting dynasty for my lord, because you fight the Lord battles, and no wrongdoing will

be found in you as long as you live. Even though someone is pursuing you to take your life, the life of my lord will be bound securely in the bundle of the living by the Lord your God, but the lives of your enemies he will hurl away as from the pocket of a sling. When the Lord has fulfilled for my lord every good thing he promised concerning him and has appointed him ruler over Israel, my lord will not have on his conscience the staggering burden of needless bloodshed or of having avenged himself. And when the Lord your God has brought my lord success, remember your servant."

David said to Abigail, "Praise be to the Lord, the God of Israel, who has sent you today to meet me. May you be blessed for your good judgment and for keeping me from bloodshed this day and from avenging myself with my own hands. Otherwise, as surely as the Lord, the God of Israel, lives, who has kept me from harming you, if you had not come quickly to meet me, not one male belonging to Nabal would have been left alive by daybreak."

1 Samuel 25:2-32

You can read the full story in 1 Samuel 25:2-44; 2 Samuel 2:2-3:3; 1 Chronicles 2:16-17.

Ever laughed when something unfortunate or funny happened to a friend? Sometimes we enjoy watching others fail. We devour news stories about the faults and failures of political leaders. Celebrity gossip magazines are among the most popular on the newsstands.

Abigail was beautiful and intelligent, but her husband, Nabal, was rich, foolish and mean. Instead of focusing on her husband's weaknesses, Abigail offset them with her strengths. She cared for those around her, supported her family and saved her household from disaster by her words and actions.

David and his men were on the run from Saul, yet they showed respect to Nabal's men by protecting their flocks from marauders. The customs of the day dictated that in return, David could expect help and hospitality from Nabal in his own time of need. Although he was hiding in caves, David was the anointed king, and as such he deserved to be treated with respect.

The time came when David asked Nabal to repay the favor. He sent ten of his men to ask for some simple provisions — bread, water and meat — as was his right according to custom. But Nabal refused David's request, insulting him with his reply, "Who is this David?" (1 Samuel 25:10). David was enraged. In his anger, he gathered his men to launch an attack, intending to kill Nabal and all the men of his household.

Abigail was trusted and respected by everyone in her husband's household. One of the servants told her of Nabal's refusal to help David and the impending slaughter.

At this point, we might forgive Abigail if she had allowed calamity to befall her cruel and foolish husband. Yet, even though she knew Nabal's character, his faults and failings, she desperately sought to protect him and his household. As a result, she saved David from the consequences of his hasty desire for revenge.

With grace and wisdom, Abigail quickly prepared a lavish gift of food for David and his men and set out to meet them. When she saw him, Abigail bowed low before David. She humbly accepted all of the blame for her husband's actions: "My lord, let the blame be on me alone." (1 Samuel 25:24 NIV84) Then she reminded David that God is the One who avenges wrongs. Her wise words and humble attitude changed David's mind and called forth the best in him. He turned from his hasty actions and repented of his wrongful desire to avenge himself; then he sent her home in peace. Abigail's household was safe, and she prevented David from wrongfully shedding blood.

God Himself dealt with Nabal's folly, striking him dead just a few days later. Meanwhile, David gave thanks to God for keeping him from doing wrong and asked Abigail to become his wife. What a change for Abigail, to go from a mean, surly fool of a husband to becoming a wife of the anointed king! Her wisdom enabled her to be a blessing to those around her.

So often we are tempted to point out the failures of those around us. Somehow it makes us feel better, even though we know that we are utterly flawed. The Bible says that Jesus died for you, and that you're a sinner who can't be perfect on your own, no matter how hard you try.

As Christ-followers, we have received such grace in our human weakness, but sometimes we are tempted to gloat rather than extend that grace to others. God has called us to be counter-cultural in our relationships with family, colleagues and those in our churches. Rather than pointing fingers or whispering behind people's backs, we are to look out and care for them.

If you live or work with people you consider foolish, ill-equipped or poorly chosen for their tasks, how do you respond? God is watching your attitude. Do you rejoice in their failures or help them by covering their failures, forgiving their shortcomings and protecting them from attack?

We all drop the ball from time to time. Those on our team — our friends, family and fellow Christians — are there to pick up the ball, place it back in our hands and encourage us to keep playing. In a dog-eat-dog world in which everyone constantly strives for success, shouldn't we be helping others succeed instead?

Some of the most successful men and women of our time failed time and time again, but had people picking them up and encouraging them to try again. Who knows what ripples one word of encouragement will send out into the world?

Jesus came to pick up every ball you're ever going to drop; He took the consequences of your failures and wrong choices on the cross. He offers forgiveness and grace to those who follow Him.

Whose team are you on? How can you support and encourage others on your team?

Standing Firm in the Face of Accusations

This is how the birth of Jesus the Messiah came about: His mother Mary was pledged to be married to Joseph, but before they came together, she was found to be pregnant through the Holy Spirit. Because Joseph her husband was faithful to the law, and yet did not want to expose her to public disgrace, he had in mind to divorce her quietly.

But after he had considered this, an angel of the Lord appeared to him in a dream and said, "Joseph son of David, do not be afraid to take Mary home as your wife, because what is conceived in her is from the Holy Spirit. She will give birth to a son, and you are to give him the name Jesus, because he will save his people from their sins."

All this took place to fulfill what the Lord had said through the prophet: "The virgin will conceive and give birth to a son, and they will call him Immanuel" (which means "God with us").

When Joseph woke up, he did what the angel of the Lord had commanded him and took Mary home as his wife. But he did

not consummate their marriage until she gave birth to a son.
And he gave him the name Jesus.

Matthew 1:18-25

For nothing is impossible with God.

Luke 1:37 (NIV84)

I'm innocent! I didn't do it! It wasn't me! Have you ever uttered any of those words? We can probably remember defending ourselves as children at home or at school. Kids can certainly be cruel, but being wrongly accused as adults can be even more difficult to deal with.

When faced with unjust accusations, it's tempting to defend ourselves in order to prove that we are in the right. When you are slandered, it's natural to want to clear your name.

Mary, Jesus' mother, was a young woman when she was faced with the worst kind of accusation. She faced total disgrace when she became pregnant by the Holy Spirit. When the angel Gabriel told this young, virgin girl that she was going to give birth to a son, Mary knew that it wouldn't be a smooth ride. She also knew that, as an unmarried mother,

her pregnancy could put her life as risk. Yet her response was, "I am the Lord's servant. May it be to me as you have said." (Luke 1:38)

There are times in our lives when we face unjust accusations. People may speak about us unfairly or whisper behind our backs. At times, God may lead us in a direction that others don't understand. We might know what God has promised or called us to, but we can't clearly see how He will work out the details in our lives (and within cultural expectations). How can we handle challenging situations and glorify God?

It may be tempting to idolize Mary and imagine her as someone very different from ourselves. Many picture her as a girl with no struggles in her heart or mind, a woman who easily overcame every difficulty and challenge. It is all too easy to see her as nothing more than a character in the Christmas story.

As a result, we tend to overlook the overwhelmingly difficult situation she faced so soon after God revealed His plan for her life. Mary had a revelation from God, who sent an angel to tell her of His amazing plan. While we may not have angels speaking to us, we do have God's Word, in the Bible, to tell us of His promises and plans for us.

Gabriel also told Mary that her cousin Elizabeth, who everyone knew was barren, was now pregnant. Soon after, Mary traveled to see Elizabeth and discovered that she was indeed pregnant, and what the angel said was true. How encouraged she must have been to realize that her experience with the angel was real and that God had truly chosen her for this special task.

When Elizabeth welcomed Mary, she did not know that Mary was pregnant, yet she spoke prophetically about the child she was carrying. God filled Elizabeth with His Holy Spirit and supernaturally spoke to Mary, just as He still fills men and women with His Holy Spirit and enables them to speak for Him. He gives prophetic words and images to convey encouragement or highlighting relevant Bible verses.

By the time Mary returned to her home town of Nazareth, her pregnancy would have started to show. On that long journey, imagine the struggles she must have gone through in her mind. She knew that she had to face those closest to her, and that they were not likely to understand or believe her incredible story.

I can imagine Mary holding onto her memory of the angel's visit and Elizabeth's inspired words as she traveled home to face looming accusations. She must have greatly feared the look on her fiancé's face when he realized that she was pregnant. And she also had to face her parents and the perceived shame she has brought upon their household. Her once-friendly neighbors would have refused to look her in the eyes. Her friends would no longer want anything to do with her. But Mary held on tight to God's promise.

She didn't know how God would work out His plan in her life, but she waited and trusted Him. She held onto the promises that God had spoken and the things she knew of His character as she walked the difficult path He had laid out for her.

God has also given you promises for your life through His Word. His promises can help you keep going when the going gets tough and the future is uncertain. Ask Him to reveal His promises to you as you read the Bible today.

What promises has God given to sustain you through difficult times?

Trusting and Being Trustworthy

In the time of Herod king of Judea there was a priest named Zechariah, who belonged to the priestly division of Abijah; his wife Elizabeth was also a descendant of Aaron. Both of them were righteous in the sight of God, observing all the Lord's commands and decrees blamelessly. But they were childless because Elizabeth was not able to conceive, and they were both very old.

Once when Zechariah's division was on duty and he was serving as priest before God, he was chosen by lot, according to the custom of the priesthood, to go into the temple of the Lord and burn incense. And when the time for the burning of incense came, all the assembled worshipers were praying outside.

Then an angel of the Lord appeared to him, standing at the right side of the altar of incense. When Zechariah saw him, he was startled and was gripped with fear. But the angel said to him: "Do not be afraid, Zechariah; your prayer has been heard. Your wife Elizabeth will bear you a son, and you are to call him John. He will be a joy and delight to you, and many will rejoice because of his birth, for he will be great in the sight of the Lord. He is never to take wine or other fermented drink, and he will be filled with the Holy Spirit even before he is born. He will bring back many of the people of Israel to the Lord their God. And he will go on before the Lord, in the spirit and power of Elijah, to turn the hearts of the parents to their children and the disobedient to the wisdom of the righteous — to make ready a people prepared for the Lord."

Zechariah asked the angel, "How can I be sure of this? I am an old man and my wife is well along in years."

The angel said to him, "I am Gabriel. I stand in the presence of God, and I have been sent to speak to you and to tell you this good news. And now you will be silent and not able to speak until the day this happens, because you did not believe my words, which will come true at their appointed time."

Meanwhile, the people were waiting for Zechariah and wondering why he stayed so long in the temple. When he came out, he could not speak to them. They realized he had seen a vision in the temple, for he kept making signs to them but remained unable to speak.

When his time of service was completed, he returned home. After this his wife Elizabeth became pregnant and for five months remained in seclusion. The Lord has done this for me," she said. "In these days he has shown his favor and taken away my disgrace among the people."

Luke 1:5-25

Blessed is she who has believed that what the Lord has said to her will be accomplished!

Luke 1:45 (NIV84)

How do you act when others are watching you? Do you act the same as you do when you're alone? Many of us, even subconsciously, tend to act a little differently when we know that our actions are being observed by others.

Elizabeth was an older woman, probably over 50, and she may have been into her eighties. An angel spoke to her husband, Zechariah, and told him that he would have a son and that he was to name him John. Zechariah asked Gabriel how this would happen, and as a result of his unbelief, he was struck dumb until John's birth.

After so many years of barrenness, Elizabeth became pregnant. She remained in seclusion for at least five months until her pregnancy was clearly showing.

Soon after, the same angel spoke to Mary, her relative, to tell her that, though a virgin, she would give birth to a son. He also told her that the child would "He will be great and will be called the son of the Most High". (Luke 1:32) Then Gabriel gave Mary some more seemingly impossible news: Elizabeth, though old and barren, was also expecting a son. The angel assured her that it was true, for "nothing is impossible with God." (Luke 1:37)

Throughout history, God has chosen many special women to fulfill His purposes. Over time, He gradually moulded and shaped each of their unique characters. Like Elizabeth, He waited to fulfill many of their dreams until they had grown older and wiser, to a point where God could trust them to fulfill His purpose. He watched them respond and act faithfully even when they thought no one was watching, and He knew that He was more important than anything else in their lives.

God trusted Elizabeth to raise John the Baptist because she had trusted Him through many trials. As a result, she had the joy of bringing up a man with an incredible destiny.

Elizabeth was also able to offer encouragement and hospitality to Mary, the mother of Jesus during the first few months of her pregnancy. God used Elizabeth to confirm what He had spoken to Mary, confirming the angel's words to her as she exclaimed, "Blessed is the child you will bear!" (Luke 1:42) At that point, it is unlikely that Mary was visibly pregnant, but the Holy Spirit filled Elizabeth and revealed this to her.

Luke tells us that Elizabeth was righteous, and that she descended from a line of priests, as did Zechariah. This means that despite her difficult situation she never sinned by accusing God. God was watching Elizabeth, even when she felt like she was alone, and even through her struggles, as she faithfully chose to trust Him.

Elizabeth lived in a society where children, especially sons, greatly influenced social status. She must have yearned and ached for a son, and the stigma of infertility would have stung daily. After years of humiliation and heartbreak, God gave her the son she had been praying for — a son who would bring her and Zechariah "joy and delight" (Luke 1:14). When Elizabeth became pregnant, the burden of barrenness was finally lifted. In her own words, God had "shown his favor and taken away my disgrace."

God richly rewards our years of faithfulness to Him. He gave Elizabeth an important role: to raise a boy who would become a prophet and prepare the way for the long-awaited Messiah.

If this were a movie, Elizabeth would not be the star of the story, but she would play a key supporting role. She strongly influenced the lives of three main characters: her son, John; her relative, Mary and Mary's son, Jesus.

Sometimes when we're expecting to play the lead role, God casts us as a member of the supporting cast. We may not think anyone is paying attention to our parts, but God is lovingly watching our every thought and action. The supporting cast is no less crucial to history's screenplay; they give the story its beautiful intricacy.

Are you called to play the lead role, or are you playing a key supporting role in your current situation?

Are you fulfilling your God-given role patiently and faithfully?

Time for Your Breakthrough Moment

*Again the Israelites did evil in the eyes of the Lord, now that
Ehud was dead. So the Lord sold them into the hands of Jabin
king of Canaan, who reigned in Hazor. Sisera, the commander
of his army, was based in Harosheth Haggoyim. Because he had
nine hundred chariots fitted with iron and had cruelly oppressed
the Israelites for twenty years, they cried to the Lord for help.*

*Now Deborah, a prophet, the wife of Lappidoth, was leading
Israel at that time. She held court under the Palm of Deborah
between Ramah and Bethel in the hill country of Ephraim, and
the Israelites went up to her to have their disputes decided.
She sent for Barak son of Abinoam from Kedesh in Naphtali
and said to him, "The Lord, the God of Israel, commands you:
'Go, take with you ten thousand men of Naphtali and Zebulun
and lead them up to Mount Tabor. I will lead Sisera, the commander of Jabin's army, with his chariots and his troops to the
Kishon River and give him into your hands."*

...

*When they told Sisera that Barak son of Abinoam had gone
up to Mount Tabor, Sisera summoned from Harosheth*

Haggoyim to the Kishon River all his men and his nine hundred chariots fitted with iron.

Then Deborah said to Barak, "Go! This is the day the Lord has given Sisera into your hands. Has not the Lord gone ahead of you?" So Barak went down Mount Tabor, with ten thousand men following him. At Barak's advance, the Lord routed Sisera and all his chariots and army by the sword, and Sisera got down from his chariot and fled on foot.

Barak pursued the chariots and army as far as Harosheth Haggoyim, and all Sisera's troops fell by the sword; not a man was left.

Judges 4:1-7; 12-16

On that day God subdued Jabin, the Canaanite king, before the Israelites. And the hand of the Israelites grew stronger and stronger against Jabin, the Canaanite king, until they destroyed him.

Judges 4:23-24 (NIV84)

Read more about the story of Deborah in Judges 4 and 5.

Ever been faced with a seemingly insurmountable obstacle? Have you prayed and prayed for a situation that seems hopeless without receiving a definite answer?

Tash suffered a post-viral illness that turned into ME, or chronic fatigue syndrome. She quickly went from being an active young woman of twenty-something living in a wheelchair and depending upon her husband to complete the household tasks. She was easily exhausted.

Over several years, Tash received prayer many times. After one occasion, she sensed her symptoms easing, so she started walking, first for just one minute each day. After a few months, she was walking an hour a day. Her symptoms had stabilized, and she was finally able to enjoy a normal life. Most of all, she enjoyed the freedom to care for her young toddler, Ben. After much waiting and persistence, God met her in her place of need, broke into her life and restored her life.

Deborah lived in a time when the Israelites faced an intimidating enemy. They had been oppressed for twenty years. Even when they entered the promised land, their foes seemed impossible to defeat; the opposing army had an impressive array of tens of thousands of men and nine hundred iron chariots.

Yet there came a day when the people cried out to the Lord, and God responded by sending word to Barak, the commander of the Israelite army, through Deborah, His prophetess. He promised that as Barak took up ten thousand men to fight, He would draw the enemy in and deliver them into the hands of the Israelites.

After twenty years of oppression and waiting, God spoke. The people responded and confronted their enemy in battle, and they fought until they were victorious. From that time on, they grew stronger and finally destroyed the king who had so cruelly oppressed them.

When God speaks, He releases power to change a situation, even if that situation has remained the same for years or decades. The story of Deborah the prophetess shows that when God speaks, we have an opportunity to respond in faith. Tash's story shows that God still supernaturally changes lives today.

A day comes when God reaches out in power to change things. His word can bring into being that which does not exist. His power can utterly destroy the works of the enemy. He can change our lives in an instant.

When we need breakthrough in our lives, we need to ask God for help. He may send someone to pray for us or to speak a prophetic word of encouragement, or highlight a Bible verse we are reading. However God speaks to us, we need respond in faith. He loves our faith, even when it is as small as a mustard seed. Knowing that God still speaks into our lives, don't wait to see what happens; find a way to step out with your mustard seed of faith and see what He will do!

Are you asking God for breakthrough today? When He starts to speak into your situation, are you ready to respond in faith?

Never Too Late to Make Your Choice

Sisera, meanwhile, fled on foot to the tent of Jael, the wife of Heber the Kenite, because there was an alliance between Jabin king of Hazor and the family of Heber the Kenite.

Jael went out to meet Sisera and said to him, "Come, my lord, come right in. Don't be afraid." So he entered her tent, and she covered him with a blanket.

"I'm thirsty," he said. "Please give me some water." She opened a skin of milk, gave him a drink, and covered him up.

"Stand in the doorway of the tent," he told her. "If someone comes by and asks you, 'Is anyone in there?' say 'No.'"

But Jael, Heber's wife, picked up a tent peg and a hammer and went quietly to him while he lay fast asleep, exhausted. She drove the peg through his temple into the ground, and he died.

Just then Barak came by in pursuit of Sisera, and Jael went out to meet him. "Come," she said, "I will show you the man you're looking for." So he went in with her, and there lay Sisera with the tent peg through his temple — dead.

On that day God subdued Jabin king of Canaan before the Israelites. And the hand of the Israelites pressed harder and harder against Jabin king of Canaan until they destroyed him.

Judges 4:17-24

...choose for yourselves this day whom you will serve, whether the gods your ancestors served beyond the Euphrates, or the gods of the Amorites, in whose land you are living. But as for me and my household, we will serve the Lord.

Joshua 24:15

You can read the full story in Judges 4.

Don't you love to celebrate when your team wins? We love to celebrate victory. In a conflict, those on the winning side are usually the only ones viewed as heroes.

But are treachery and heroism really so different? In times of war, what seems like treachery to the losing nation is often viewed as heroism to those on the winning side. Does your view depend which side you're on? As Christ-followers, we have many opportunities to choose sides throughout our lives.

Jael was an outsider, not a part of the Israelite nation, yet God used this unlikely woman to bring Israel victory over its oppressor.

A man named Sisera led the Canaanite army in the battle against the Israelites. Following Canaan's defeat, Sisera fled on foot and sought refuge in a friend's camp. He was welcomed by his friend's wife, Jael, who looked after him. She gave him milk and covered him with a warm blanket. Overtaken by the exhaustion of the battle, Sisera fell asleep.

The violence of what happened next may be unpleasant for our modern minds to visualize. Jael took one of the massive pegs used to stabilize the tent and hammered it right through Sisera's temple, killing him instantly. She used a tool that she was familiar with, as it was the women's role in those days to pitch the tents. The tent peg was heavy and probably well over thirty centimeters long, but her muscles were well accustomed to wielding its weight.

How did Sisera manage to flee the battlefield unharmed after all of his ten thousand men were defeated? Maybe God allowed him to escape because He wanted to show His power. Instead of being defeated by a mighty army, Sisera was defeated by Jael, a woman and foreigner. God used her to single-handedly bring the long-awaited relief to His oppressed people.

We read that Jael's husband had moved away from the rest of his tribe. As a friend of Sisera, he may even have been making and supplying Israel's enemies with their weapons and armor. Although he was a descendent of Moses, it seems he had long since fallen away from following the God of Israel. Yet his wife, when faced with a day of choice made a courageous decision to break with the allegiance of those around her and to follow and serve the God of Israel.

Jael displayed determination and courage. Deborah called her "most blessed of women," a phrase only used elsewhere in the Bible to describe Jesus' mother, Mary.

When Jael went out to meet Sisera, she welcomed him. She made him comfortable enough to fall asleep; then she literally struck a blow for the freedom of the Israelites. God's ways are so different from our own. He rejoices in giving victory to the unlikely, weak and oppressed. He loves to use the weak to shame the strong (1 Corinthians 1:27). He can use anyone, even the most unlikely woman, to bring victory.

Jael was faced with a choice: Offer hospitality to a man who had oppressed Israel for twenty years, or change sides and end Israel's oppression. She chose wisely.

Just as she had a choice to make, we often face the choice to go the way of the world or to courageously go God's way.

Whatever capacity you serve in, God has a purpose for you. He will use your gifts, even if they seem different or unusual. He can use your strengths and talents to bring victory and blessing into your life and the lives of others.

We're all part of God's story; we're making History.

Will you courageously choose God's way rather than the world's way?

How will you play your part today?

Responding to God's Unique Calling

One of those listening was a woman named Lydia, a dealer in purple cloth from the city of Thyatira, who was a worshiper of God. The Lord opened her heart to respond to Paul's message. When she and the members of her household were baptized, she invited us to her home. "If you consider me a believer in the Lord", she said, "come and stay at my house." And she persuaded us.

Acts 16:14-15 (NIV84)

Have you ever jumped off a diving board? While you're in the air, you're totally dry, but your body will soon inevitably plunge into the water. Once you jump, you have irrevocably committed yourself to getting very wet in a very short amount of time.

How do approach the water? You can choose to sit on the edge of the swimming pool, testing the temperature before you commit to diving in, but then you will never experience the exhilaration of diving into the pool. Allowing your fear to determine your actions can deprive you of the fullness of joy.

In the same way, we can either be involved in or committed to the life of our church. We can be afraid of jumping in, unsure of what that will look like for us.

Real commitment comes at a cost, whether the cost is our time, energy or money. Commitment is like jumping into the pool; it's a choice that we make to wholeheartedly be a part of something.

Lydia was a business woman whose life was radically changed by an encounter with Jesus. Lydia listened, heard and responded, following Jesus without hesitation. Like Lydia, we should make commitments based on our hearts' responses to Jesus

Lydia was from Thyatira in Asia. She had travelled several hundred miles to live and work in the European city of Philippi. It is possible that she moved away from her hometown to find a different way of life. Thyatira was a thriving business center, but there was one problem: Acceptance and success as an artisan was dependent upon belonging to the guilds, and membership in the guilds meant worshipping the sun god, participating in orgies and other forms of sexual immorality.

We do know that Lydia "sold purple". A modern-day equivalent may be a sales associate for designer clothing. Purple signified wealth, and people who couldn't afford an entire purple garment would sew on a small patch of the rich color to indicate financial success.

One day, Lydia had a divine appointment. Paul came to speak to a small crowd outside the city gate, and Lydia sat among them with the right heart and attitude. As she heard the truth for the first time, she didn't wait to see how the other women would respond. With her mind made up, she wholeheartedly became a committed Christ-follower, and her life was forever changed.

Lydia didn't stop at accepting that her sins were forgiven by Jesus and being baptized; she was happy and eager to serve in whatever capacity she could. Her faith turned into action as she opened her home first to Paul and Luke, then to other believers as the church grew.

Yet there was a real cost to Lydia's obedience: It put her at a high risk of persecution. She welcomed Paul and Silas into her home after they were imprisoned for teaching about Jesus. The first few Christians in Philippi likely gathered there too, and they were a diverse and unlikely group of people, including a woman who had been possessed by demons and Paul's jailer and his family. This was certainly an interesting mix of people for Lydia to welcome into her home!

Lydia didn't hesitate, she jumped right in. She was fully committed, loving God and serving the church in her city. What could God do through us if we responded to and served Him as wholeheartedly as Lydia did?

As a Christ-follower, are you committed, or just involved?

How is your heart attitude? Is there anything holding you back from responding to God's life-changing love?

Straight to the Heart of the Issue

As Jesus and his disciples were on their way, he came to a village where a woman named Martha opened her home to him. She had a sister called Mary, who sat at the Lord's feet listening to what he said. But Martha was distracted by all the preparations that had to be made. She came to him and asked, "Lord, don't you care that my sister has left me to do the work by myself? Tell her to help me!"

"Martha, Martha," the Lord answered, "you are worried and upset about many things, but few things are needed — or indeed only one. Mary has chosen what is better, and it will not be taken away from her."

Luke 10:38-42

The Lord disciplines those he loves, as a father the son he delights in.

Proverbs 3:12

You can read more about Jesus and Mary in John 11 and 12:2.

It isn't fair! No one else is working as hard as me! Why isn't anyone helping? Why are things always left to me?

When we're busy and tired, it can be infuriating to watch others who could help us choose not to. We tend to focus on how unfair life is. Sometimes we bottle up our feelings until we explode with angry words or actions.

This is the situation Martha faced when Jesus and the crowd that followed Him came to visit her home. Jesus never arrived on His own; He was usually surrounded by his twelve disciples as well as others who followed Him.

It is important to understand that Martha had a special place in Jesus' heart. She wasn't just a follower of Jesus; she was His friend, and He loved her as a sister. It was to Martha's home that Jesus went when He needed rest. But she was like Peter in that she was a bit outspoken and impulsive.

When Martha confronted Jesus about Mary's apparent laziness, He did not condemn her; He saw into her heart and knew that the issue was a wrong attitude in her heart. He took the opportunity to teach her, as He did so often with His disciples..

Jesus spoke so gently that He touched the very heart of the issue: Martha had allowed her heart to become bitter and resentful. Her to-do list seemed endless. Though she loved to spend time with Him, Jesus came to her home with all His followers, and she felt overwhelmed.

Martha's issue wasn't that she was serving too much, but that she allowed her ministry to Jesus to become a chore. She had begun to resent her sister, who simply enjoyed spending time with Jesus. She allowed her gift of service to become more important than spending time with Him. After all, everyone else was only sitting and listening to Him.

Things probably started out great for Martha, who genuinely welcomed Jesus into her home and graciously served Him as an act of love and friendship. But as people praised her for being such a welcoming host, she must have felt increasing pressure to perform well. Perhaps she slipped into thinking that Jesus loved her not for herself, but because she was such a good host. What started out as a good thing, humble service to Jesus became more important than being a good friend to Him.

As we serve our families and churches, we too can easily lose sight of what is truly important. We can quickly move from serving because we love others to serving because we want to be loved. We may think that our role has more value than someone else's, yet the Bible tells us that we all have a part to play in the body of Christ, and that everyone's gifts are equally important (Romans 12:4-8). We must not forget the simple truth that, as Christ-followers, we are all sinners — forgiven, loved and accepted by a gracious God.

As busy Christian women, it is possible for us to do the right things with the wrong attitudes. Sometimes we take on more tasks than Jesus has asked us to. The honest truth is that your to-do list may never get finished. It's only God's to-do list that always gets completed.

Martha thought that serving Jesus was more important than spending time with Jesus. She was so afraid of disappointing Him that she forgot to relax and enjoy spending time with Him. We can easily fall into the same trap today.

Have you ever felt that your role in the church is indispensable? What would fall apart if you left? Are you really the only person who can fill that role? Do you see a hierarchy of strengths, with one gift being more special than another, or do you value everyone's gifts?

God loves and accepts you completely today. He delights in you. You are the apple of His eye.

As a Christ-follower, you don't have to do anything to earn His love or approval.

You don't have to be afraid of disappointing Jesus. As a Christ-follower He fully accepts and perfectly loves you. How does this truth change your approach to life today?

True Worshippers

Then Mary took about a pint of pure nard, an expensive per-
fume; she poured it on Jesus' feet and wiped his feet with her
hair. And the house was filled with the fragrance of the per-
fume.

John 12:3

You can read more of this story in Luke 10:38-42;
John 11:1-44; 12:1-11.

**Can you remember a time when you suddenly understood some-
thing for the first time?** Have you experienced that "Aha!" moment
when the lights finally seem to come on?

When we come to a place of understanding, it's as if someone has
switched the light on and we can see clearly. We can never go back

to the moment when we lacked understanding; our world is forever changed.

Mary of Bethany listened to Jesus and recognized who He was, and she was also one of the few individuals who caught a glimpse of where He was going. While sitting at Jesus' feet and listening to His words, Mary realized who He was, it was her "aha" moment. Her life was never the same again. As a result, her heart was fully committed to Him, and her feelings overflowed in the form of extravagant worship.

Mary knew that Jesus truly loved and accepted her, and the security of that knowledge gave her the courage to break with Jewish customs in order to express her love for Him. She chose not to go unnoticed in a society where women were often unseen. She dared to be different because she wasn't afraid of being ridiculed or misunderstood. And she spared no expense as she poured out her best perfume, worth a year's salary, on Jesus' feet. She also defied social convention, letting her hair down in the presence of men to dry Jesus' feet in her worship of Him.

Is our culture so very different from Mary's? We are often afraid to act because we worry about what people might think or say. We may fear openly voicing our beliefs because we may be ridiculed. We shy away from radical action, afraid of being misunderstood.

Mary recognized that Jesus was the Son of God, and this truth transformed her life. She knew Him as a friend, and His love for her changed her heart and eradicated any fear.

This picture of Mary pouring out her perfume as an act of love is a pale forerunner of how Jesus poured out His life for us. He spared no expense in purchasing our freedom. He set us free from our sins, our fears and the world's expectations. If we could somehow grasp all that Jesus did for us, how would we respond to such extravagant love?

Knowing God's love and acceptance empowers us to be confident and step into a world of need. It enables us to lay down our lives as worship before Him.

Is it your experience to know Jesus as your friend?

In what way is Jesus calling you to stand out from the crowd and be different?

Faith for Life's Challenges and Trials

Now a man of the tribe of Levi married a Levite woman, and she became pregnant and gave birth to a son. When she saw that he was a fine child, she hid him for three months. But when she could hide him no longer, she got a papyrus basket for him and coated it with tar and pitch. Then she placed the child in it and put it among the reeds along the bank of the Nile. His sister stood at a distance to see what would happen to him.

Then Pharaoh's daughter went down to the Nile to bathe, and her attendants were walking along the riverbank. She saw the basket among the reeds and sent her female slave to get it. She opened it and saw the baby. He was crying, and she felt sorry for him. "This is one of the Hebrew babies," she said.

Then his sister asked Pharaoh's daughter, "Shall I go and get one of the Hebrew women to nurse the baby for you?"

"Yes, go," she answered. So the girl went and got the baby's mother. Pharaoh's daughter said to her, "Take this baby and

nurse him for me, and I will pay you." So the woman took the baby and nursed him. When the child grew older, she took him to Pharaoh's daughter and he became her son. She named him Moses, saying, "I drew him out of the water."

Exodus 2:1-8

By faith Moses' parents hid him for three months after he was born, because they saw he was no ordinary child, and they were not afraid of the king's edict.

Hebrews 11:23

You can read the full story in Exodus 1; 2:8-10; 6:19-20; 11:23; Numbers 26:59 and Micah 6:4.

Do you love or hate suspenseful movies? Do you enjoy sitting on the edge of your seat in anticipation? Or do you check out the final page of a book before you read it to find out how it ends?

We long to know how our lives will turn out, but God rarely allows us to flip to the last page ahead of time. Sometimes we have to take leaps of faith.

When we're faced with challenges, it's tempting to think that that the problems we face are impossible to conquer. There are times when we face a choice in the midst of trials: to trust God, or rely on our own strength. We have an opportunity to exercise our faith so that it is stretched, and we grow. Of course, it wouldn't be faith if we knew the outcome in advance.

Jochebed and her husband must have been excited at the prospect of having another child, yet they also must have feared the arrival of a son. Pharaoh had decreed genocide upon the Hebrew nation; every male newborn was being abducted and thrown into the Nile. The penalty for disobedience was death.

By the grace of God, Jochebed managed to hide her pregnancy and the birth of her child. She hid her baby boy for three months before she had to take action. As she wove the basket that would carry her baby, she must have fervently prayed for God to show her a way to save him. Maybe she thought, "perhaps the Lord will act in our behalf" (1 Samuel 14:6) as she placed her son in the basket among the reeds. Could she have imagined that one day God would use this tiny child to save her people?

How do you think Jochebed and her daughter, Miriam, felt as they sent the baby down to the river? We don't read of tears or hysterics;

rather, there is a sense of peace as they stepped out to trust God. Their faith was somehow stronger than their fears.

As she courageously sacrificed her rights as a mother and let go of her baby son, God turned the situation around completely. He placed the child in his mother's care and even arranged for Pharaohs' daughter to pay her to nurse him. Imagine the joy and love Jochebed must have felt as the details of this plan unfolded. Just as Abraham gave up his son, Isaac, only to receive him back, Jochebed courageously placed her baby in the river, only to be commanded to care for him by the same royal family who sought to slaughter him. Oh, the incredible, beautiful irony, as Pharaoh's daughter placed Moses in his mother's arms and offered to pay her to nurse him.

As we read the familiar story of Moses, assured in advance of the happy ending. We know that Pharaohs' daughter will discover and rescue the baby in the papyrus basket, feel sorry for him and adopt him as her son.

It is easy to forget that Moses' mother had no such reassuring knowledge about the end of the story. Everything Jochebed did was purely an act of faith; she placed complete trust in God.

In today's world, we often hear and read about God moving in miraculous ways, still we tend to struggle to trust in His provision. How much more would Jochebed have struggled? She knew the stories of her ancestors, even of her grandfather Jacob, yet she had not seen God intervene during her lifetime. She could have chosen to believe that God had abandoned her people to suffer under the Egyptians' rule.

Jochebed made a choice to trust God with her son, whom she knew was no ordinary child. We can look back through history and see that he was indeed a child with an incredible destiny, yet Moses' parents had only a glimmer of hope. Their faith ultimately resulted in the rescue of the entire Hebrew nation from slavery, and Jochebed's heroic actions have inspired and encouraged women for centuries.

So, just what is faith? The Bible tells us that "faith is being sure of what we hope for and certain of what we do not see" (Hebrews 11:1).

Faith is stepping out into the unknown, knowing that we can trust the One who holds our futures in His hands. Faith trusts our loving Father to lead us into His good purposes and plans for our life. Faith believes that He will work all things together for our good.

What areas of your life do you need to entrust to God today?

Two Women, Two Choices

Now when Athaliah the mother of Ahaziah saw that her son was dead, she arose and destroyed all the royal family. But Jehosheba, the daughter of King Joram, sister of Ahaziah, took Joash the son of Ahaziah and stole him away from among the king's sons who were being put to death, and she put him and his nurse in a bedroom. Thus they hid him from Athaliah, so that he was not put to death. And he remained with her six years, hidden in the house of the Lord, while Athaliah reigned over the land.

2 Kings 11:1-3, ESV

You can read more of this story in 2 Chronicles 22
and 2 Kings 11.

Ever hoped a distant relative would leave you a million-dollar inheritance? Or thought of what you might spend an unexpected fortune on? World travel, a new home, the fulfillment of a long-awaited dream? Whether financial or spiritual, our lives and choices leave a legacy for those who come after us.

Jehosheba was a sister of the king and a member of the royal family. She was married to the high priest, Jehoiada. Despite the deep sin of her society, and even the sin of her own family, she chose to follow and worship the one true God, and she lived a righteous life.

In contrast, Athaliah was a follower of foreign gods and an idol-worshipper. She was a daughter of the notorious Jezebel and mother to the reigning king; she too was a member of the royal family. Athaliah used the death of her son to seize power and claim the throne. On hearing that her son was dead, she ruthlessly had every male heir killed. This may have involved murdering her own sons and certainly those of the other royal wives.

The contrast between these two women clearly shows that our choices — not our pasts, societies or families — determine who we are. Both women were royal, born into privilege, but each made very different choices.

Jehosheba rescued the baby prince, Joash, from slaughter by Athaliah. She hid him and his wet nurse in a bedroom. Then she took him safely to the temple, where she and her husband hid him for a period of six years.

Jehosheba saw the sin of her nation but wasn't tainted by it. She seized the opportunity to save her nephew at the risk of great personal danger. She was wise to hide his nurse as well so that she could care for and feed him.

After six years of hiding, Jehosheba's husband, the high priest, deemed it time to anoint Joash and proclaim him king. After living under the oppression of Athaliah, the nation rejoiced that a true king had survived, and they welcomed him to his rightful place on the throne. The traitor and murderer, Athaliah, was finally put to death. God used one woman in His eternal plan to thwart the actions of an evil one.

Athaliah and Jehosheba provide a sobering example of two women whose choices and actions drastically changed the future. One grasped at power and lost it when her false gods failed her. The other unknowingly held the fate of generations in her hands, and she did what she could to counter the evil in her society. Both had royal blood; both had parents who were foolish and wicked, and each chose her own path. The first left a legacy of wickedness, the second a legacy of righteousness.

Jehosheba probably could not have imagined the massive impact of her actions through the ages. The infant Prince Joash was the only remaining boy in the royal line of David. When she saved that baby's life, she preserved a bloodline of kings and allowed the Bible prophecies about the Messiah being descended from King David to be fulfilled many years later.

Your past or background doesn't dictate who you are. If you have accepted Christ as your Savior, He has made you a new creation (2 Corinthians 5:17). The old has gone, and the new has come. A new life has been given to you. The Holy Spirit empowers you and gives you the wisdom and strength to make Godly choices. You have a hope and a future (Jeremiah 29:11).

Jehosheba saw what was happening in her nation, and she did what she could, countering evil with good. She left a legacy of righteousness, ingenuity, patience, courage and faith.

What kind of legacy will you leave? Are there any changes God is directing you to make?

A Trusted and Beloved Servant

"I commend to you our sister Phoebe, who is a servant of the church which is at Cenchrea; that you receive her in the Lord in a manner worthy of the saints, and that you help her in whatever matter she may have need of you; for she herself has also been a helper of many, and of myself as well."

Romans 16:1-2, NASB

What pivotal moments in your life can you remember? Perhaps a special birthday, a wedding or a birth? Maybe the loss of a loved one or an illness? Do you remember where you were on important days in history, such as the destruction wrought on 9/11? We all have days we remember, some for good reasons and some for bad.

Phoebe could clearly remember the day she first heard about Jesus. Her life was radically changed when she understood the good news of what He had done for her, and she responded to His love and received His forgiveness.

This radical change is something that is still clearly seen in the lives of believers today. When you truly realize what God has done for you, His love, grace and forgiveness begin to transform every area of your life. They impact your time, your worship, your love, your joy, your giving and your service. As we are called to belong to Jesus, so we are called to serve, not as a duty, but as a worshipful outpouring of changed hearts and lives.

Phoebe was a member of the early church in Corinth, a diverse collection of individuals with an assortment of backgrounds and ethnicities. At the end of his letter to the church in Rome, Paul commended Phoebe.

In many ways, Phoebe was an ordinary woman. She was probably wealthy, yet she was happy to be a servant of Christ, and she used her gifts to serve the church. She didn't just donate money, she was personally involved; she saw and met the needs of individuals in an effective and practical way. Many also believe that Phoebe personally delivered Paul's letter to the Romans, undertaking a long and dangerous journey to bless and serve Paul and to encourage the church in Rome.

Jesus said, "the Son of Man did not come to be served, but to serve" (Matthew 20:29) and Paul spoke of himself as a servant (Titus 1:1), so Phoebe understood that serving was an honorable position. She did not seek titles or accolades, but found opportunities to help many in her church and city. In return for helping others, she reaped what she sowed, as Paul asked the church in Rome to help her in any matter she might need.

Phoebe was a woman confident in her identity. She was called a sister of Paul, and he fully accepted her even though she was probably a Gentile and Paul was a Jew. She would have heard Paul talk about "God our Father" (2 Thessalonians 1:1) and understood that God was her loving Father, approachable and faithful. And she poured God's love out in worshipful service to the saints in Corinth.

In a diverse community of believers, Phoebe understood that God favors equally. Her simple, faithful acts earned her Paul's trust and friendship, and all we know about her life is summed up in the two sentences at the end of a letter written by her friend. We learn much about her servant heart and her love for Jesus and His church.

If someone was to sum up your life in a single sentence, what might they say?

Embracing Your Identity in God

One day Elisha went to Shunem. And a well-to-do woman was there, who urged him to stay for a meal. So whenever he came by, he stopped there to eat. She said to her husband, "I know that this man who often comes our way is a holy man of God. Let's make a small room on the roof and put in it a bed and a table, a chair and a lamp for him. Then he can stay there whenever he comes to us."

One day when Elisha came, he went up to his room and lay down there. He said to his servant Gehazi, "Call the Shunammite." So he called her, and she stood before him. Elisha said to him, "Tell her, 'You have gone to all this trouble for us. Now what can be done for you? Can we speak on your behalf to the king or the commander of the army?'"

She replied, "I have a home among my own people."

"What can be done for her?" Elisha asked.

Gehazi said, "She has no son, and her husband is old."

Then Elisha said, "Call her." So he called her, and she stood in the doorway. "About this time next year," Elisha said, "you will hold a son in your arms."

"No, my lord!" she objected. "Please, man of God, don't mislead your servant!"

But the woman became pregnant, and the next year about that same time she gave birth to a son, just as Elisha had told her.

2 Kings 4:8-17

You can read more of this story in 2 Kings 4 and 2 Kings 8:1-6.

I have learned to be content whatever the circumstances. I know what it is to be in need, and I know what it is to have plenty. I have learned the secret of being content in any and every situation, whether well fed or hungry, whether living in plenty or in want. I can do everything through him who gives me strength.

Philippians 4:11-13

Have you ever felt like you're the only one carrying a difficult burden? Or thought that if just one thing would happen to change your circumstances, you could finally know true happiness?

It's easy to look at others and think they have it easy in comparison to our situations. Our emotions often prompt us to voice our problems. If we have a need, we may be quick to let people know how we are feeling.

The Shunammite woman had learned contentment despite her life's difficulties. She provided a place of rest and refreshment for the prophet Elisha, and in so doing, she brought him honor in Shunem, her hometown. She served him in a very practical way and, with her husband's approval, built an annex where he could stay during his visits.

The Shunammite woman saw the bigger picture of what was happening spiritually in her nation, and she chose to serve God's prophet rather than conform to society's expectations. In her culture, a woman's worth was largely determined by how many sons she bore. But despite the fact that she had no sons, we read that she was a "notable" (2 Kings 4:8, NKJV) woman. This infers that she was influential, probably wealthy and clearly of good character. Yet she did not allow her wealth or position of influence to deceive her.

Nor did this woman allow her life to be dictated by her circumstance. Her life was not characterized by anger or bitterness, but by trust and faith. She did not serve Elisha in order to earn approval or love. Rather, she served out of a place of love and acceptance. She knew that she was loved and accepted by her husband and, most importantly, by God Himself.

What is quite astonishing in this story is that, despite his regular visits to her home, Elisha had no idea that this woman's deeply desired to have a son; God had to reveal that through Gehazi. This indicates that she never dropped a hint to Elisha that she had no children or that she and her husband would love to have a son.

Paradoxically, in the midst of her longing, this woman knew a deep sense of contentment. Peace had become a part of her character, as surely as the persevering faith and tenacious trust that we see displayed in her life.

She learned to overcome challenges and say, "everything is all right" (2 Kings 4:26). Despite the whispers of neighbors and family, she had found true contentment. When Elisha asked her, "what can be done for you?" (2 Kings 4:13) her humble answer showed that she believed she had everything she needed.

One day, Elisha realized all the trouble that this woman had gone to on his behalf, and he asked his servant, Gehazi, what he could do for her in return. With a tip from Gehazi, Elisha prophesied that, though her husband was old, the Shunammite woman would give birth to a son within a year's time. The following year, she held the baby boy that she had longed for in her arms.

Strange, isn't it, that this woman gave up that which she didn't need — her wealth — to bless the man of God; in return, she received what she desired most — the gift of a son. She had everything she needed, yet God blessed her with what she wanted.

The Apostle Paul said that he learned the secret of contentment through his experiences of wealth and poverty. Yet we often strive to change our circumstances in order to achieve contentment, rather than change our hearts and minds to find contentment in the midst of our circumstances. We need to come to a point where we can say, "everything is all right" no matter what is happening because we know and trust a loving God.

Are you striving to earn His love and acceptance or serving because you are loved and accepted by God?

Can you truly say "Everything is all right"? Are you learning to be content whatever your circumstances?

Fully Unwrapping Your Gifts

In Joppa there was a disciple named Tabitha (in Greek, her name is Dorcas); she was always doing good and helping the poor. About this time she became ill and died. Her body was washed for burial and laid in an upstairs room. But the believers had heard that Peter was nearby at Lydda, so they sent two men to beg him, "Please come as soon as possible!"

So Peter returned with them; and as soon as he arrived, they took him to the upstairs room. The room was filled with widows who were weeping and showing him the coats and other clothes Dorcas had made for them. But Peter asked them all to leave the room; then he knelt and prayed. Turning to the body he said, "Get up, Tabitha." And she opened her eyes! When she saw Peter, she sat up! He gave her his hand and helped her up. Then he called in the widows and all the believers, and he presented her to them alive.

The news spread through the whole town, and many believed in the Lord.

Acts 9:36-42

In the same way, faith by itself, if it is not accompanied by action, is dead.

James 2:17

Do you love seeing Christmas presents under the tree each year? Do you enjoy opening gifts that family and friends have chosen for you? They may not always be exactly what we wanted, but each has been thoughtfully picked out with us in mind.

It's much the same when God gives us spiritual and practical gifts. Sometimes we're unsure why He has given them, but He intends for them to be used to build up the church and to encourage those around us.

Tabitha, also known as Dorcas, understood that it was important not to neglect her gifts. She happily served the widows in her community, spinning and sewing garments to keep them clothed and warm.

We are introduced to Dorcas as a disciple who lived to imitate Jesus, her teacher. The Bible tells us that she was "always doing good and helping the poor" (Acts 9:36), yet she didn't find her identity in what she did, but in who she was — a follower of Jesus. Dorcas modeled God's love for the women around her. She was dedicated, selfless and generous with her time and limited resources. She did what she could, not turning away the needy, but helping however she could.

As a woman with some resources, she could have just donated to a few good causes in her town. Instead, she chose to address the suffering of the vulnerable and poor in her community in a practical way, getting her hands dirty in the process. Consequently, she was well-loved and respected, with many good friends.

When Dorcas became sick and died, her friends sent two men to Peter, who was just a few miles away, to ask him to come at once. That Peter came so quickly says much about her character. He prayed for Dorcas, just as he had seen Jesus pray for a little girl once, and she was raised from the dead.

Sometimes the needs in our communities seem overwhelming; we may feel like the little help we could offer is just a drop in an ocean. Yet how many charities started with one person who was willing to do what they could to help, and God generously multiplied their workers and resources? Every godly work starts with one person taking a step of faith, getting out of their comfort zone and trusting God.

Dorcas gave simply and kindly, providing coats and garments, helping the poor and offering friendship. Yet there was something about the way that she lived that made the thought of living without her impossible for her circle of friends. Maybe it was her gentle and quiet spirit (1 Peter 3:4), the dignity and honor she brought to lives full of shame, or simply her positive attitude as she did everything in the name of Jesus (Col 3:17). Maybe it was the way that everything she did seemed infused with love.

Dorcas was someone who didn't hesitate to offer what she had. The Bible tells us that we have each been given gifts to serve and bless one another (1 Peter 4:10).

What gifts has God given you to serve your church and local community?

How is God calling you to get out of your comfort zone and use your gifts for His glory?

A Woman Who Holds Nothing Back

Just then he looked up and saw the rich people dropping offerings in the collection plate. Then he saw a poor widow put in two pennies. He said, "The plain truth is that this widow has given by far the largest offering today. All these others made offerings that they'll never miss; she gave extravagantly what she couldn't afford — she gave her all!"

Luke 21:1-4, The Message

Have you ever spent ages looking at one of those puzzle pictures trying to see a hidden image? Or tediously picked out the hidden words on a word search? It's a curious fact that sometimes we simply can't see what's right in front of our faces.

In Jesus' time, the religious leaders walked through the busy temple courts daily, but their vision was blinkered. They were preoccupied with spending time with other religious people, earning favor and building up their positions in the community. They often saw only what they could criticize and condemn.

That is the exact opposite of what Jesus did when He and His disciples walked through the busy temple courts. There would have been throngs of people, yet Jesus noticed one woman who was practically invisible to the rest of society. A widow, she was neglected by the religious leaders, vulnerable to exploitation, and totally dependent on others for her needs.

As the religious leaders collected money for the upkeep of the temple, they neglected the very people God wanted them to care for: the orphan and widow (Psalm 146:9). These religious people were more concerned about the approval of others, their positions of power, their fancy clothes and their bank account balances than the people God had called them to help. These men regarded the widow as the lowest of the low, unworthy of their notice. Yet Jesus not only noticed her, He stopped to honor her. He saw that her giving came from a pure, faithful heart. Because she understood that her value came from God, she generously poured out all she had in thanksgiving, holding nothing back.

In contrast, the religious leaders gave out of their excess. Their giving looked generous to others, but everything they did was about appearance. They did not understand true generosity, in which there is a cost to your own standard of living or lifestyle. In the verses that precede the story of the widow, Jesus warned His followers to "Beware!" of religious leaders, and not to become blinded like them.

Even when we start to understand God's grace to us, it's easy to allow small things to work their way under our skin. We tend to criticize, moan or become impatient or jealous when people don't meet our expectations. We easily become self-centered, focusing on our own needs and well-being, rather than embracing self-denial and allowing God to use our gifts and resources to change the world. We need to constantly be on the lookout for anything that leads us away from God's grace and learn to rely on Him, enjoying His love and approval.

True religion begins with grace. Under the law we got the punishment we deserved, but Jesus took that punishment and we are accepted by God, through His son. Grace is unfair, it's outrageous.

Once you grasp the incredible and outrageous grace of God, there is only one response, the wholehearted giving of your life back to Him.

Have you allowed God's grace to touch your heart?

Are you able to give freely and extravagantly, or is something holding you back?

Faithful in Trials and Humiliation

After this, Jesus traveled about from one town and village to another, proclaiming the good news of the kingdom of God. The Twelve were with him, and also some women who had been cured of evil spirits and diseases: Mary (called Magdalene) from whom seven demons had come out; Joanna the wife of Chuza, the manager of Herod's household; Susanna; and many others. These women were helping to support them out of their own means.

Luke 8:1-3

Blessed is the one who perseveres under trial because, having stood the test, that person will receive the crown of life that the Lord has promised to those who love him.

James 1:12

Do you live in fear of something? Cancer? Depression? Poverty? We can often hide these fears deep down and wonder if God will sustain us during challenging times.

When we look at how different individuals handle difficulty, we can see how God sustains them. We don't always notice those who support them through those trials, but behind many sick or struggling people are friends who help and encourage them — individuals who offer practical support and loving kindness. Good friends over look the humiliations suffered and stand firm through all, in spite of their own weaknesses.

Mary Magdalene offered such friendship to Jesus. She was not only there for Him in His final hours of life, but also in the grim preparations for burial that followed His death.

The Bible says that seven demons were cast out of Mary, so we know that Jesus had miraculously healed her. Once she found His mercy, it seems Mary never looked back. She became one of His most devoted followers and contributed to His financial needs out of her own means.

Mary Magdalene spent time with Jesus, listened to His teaching and became His close friend. She was one of a handful of individuals who witnessed His harrowing crucifixion, solemn burial and glorious resurrection.

When she arrived at Jesus' tomb in the dark, ready to anoint and wash His body, she was greeted by angels who told her that Jesus was not dead; He had risen. In a time when women were regarded as second-class citizens, Jesus showed Himself to Mary on the morning of His resurrection.

While we know little of her story, we do know that Mary was not focused on her own suffering or trials. She was faithful friend to Jesus during His time of trial. Even after His death, she continued to minister to Him, purchasing expensive spices to anoint His body.

Her devotion was anything but simple. She was constant and committed, practical, thankful and steadfast. After many of Jesus' disciples fled, Mary Magdalene stayed with Him during the hardest hours of His life as He hung and died on a Roman cross.

In a modern world where decision-making seems to be governed by, "If it feels good, do it," this dedicated woman's life shows us a completely different set of priorities. It certainly would not have been a pleasure to watch her dear friend suffer incredible abuse, or His broken body being placed in a cold tomb. There was no joy in washing His lifeless body. But Mary set aside her own emotions for the benefit of her Lord. She was faithful, self-sacrificing and committed — a model of the friend that Jesus calls us to be.

In a society that feels entitled to success and health, it can be challenging when our friends experience difficult times or fall ill. We may be tempted to hold back from being the faithful friends that they need because we're not sure what to say or whether we can be of much help.

In their times of trial, Mary's example encourages us to be there for our friends when they are going through difficult times, even if it means stepping out of our comfort zones and becoming emotionally vulnerable.

A good friend stays with you in the good times and the bad times. How can you be a good friend to someone who is going through a trial or sickness?

Our Response to Circumstances

"I will do whatever you say," Ruth answered.

Ruth 3:5

All of you, clothe yourselves with humility toward one another, because, "God opposes the proud but shows favor to the humble."

Luke 8:42-48

What song would you want to play at your funeral? Apparently many people are now choosing the song, "My Way" to express their individuality, even in death. Some individuals are proud to do whatever they choose with their lives, no matter the effect their choices have on those around them.

The Bible tells us that living God's way is the only way to experience true life, and that we ought to give up our lives for others (1 John 3:16 NLT), as this brings the fulfillment we seek. God greatly values humility and the ability to learn, grow and change. We have much to learn from older and wiser Christian women, they can become a valuable part of our journey and help us to understand and grow in wisdom.

We often think that our circumstances mould our characters and are the keys in shaping who we become, but the Bible tells us that it is our characters that determine our responses to circumstances. This means that the same set of circumstances inspire one person to faith and provoke another to bitterness.

The story of Ruth is perhaps one of the most well-known in the Bible, but because we are so familiar with Ruth's story, we can miss the gravity of the pain she faced during her life.

Ruth married a foreign man who came to her country because of famine in his hometown. When Ruth married, her father-in-law was already dead, which left her mother-in-law, Naomi, a widow in a strange town. The responsibility of providing for Naomi would have fallen on Ruth's husband and his brother, who was also married. After ten years of marriage, Ruth's husband and his brother both died, leaving three widows with no provider.

Naomi, Ruth and Orpah tried to eke out a living on their own. We don't know how, but it seems possible that Ruth played a key role in providing for the three of them, while also living with the stigma of barrenness and widowhood.

Imagine for a moment that, after ten years of childless marriage, your husband died, leaving you on your own. Having run your own home and knowing the joy and security of marriage, you are reduced to living off handouts from family and friends.

When Naomi heard that the famine in her hometown had finally ended, she decided to return home, and everything changed. Ruth had become so close to her mother-in-law that she preferred to live with her than with her own family. She was not bitter, had not hardened her heart; instead, she remained full of love as she expressed her desire to follow both Naomi and her God back to her home.

Later in the story, Ruth boldly followed Naomi's wisdom, which resulted in a new marriage to a good man named Boaz.

Faced with similar circumstances, most of us would probably be tempted to sink into self-pity. We might bemoan our fates, harden our hearts and become bitter toward God for allowing tragedy and difficulties to disrupt our lives. Yet Ruth responded quite differently: She chose to trust in the God of Israel.

Whatever our age , regardless of what has happened in our lives and however much we think we know, God wants us to remain teachable. He continues to lead and teach us, gently shaping and refining our characters. Rather than stunted trees, He wants to grow us into "oaks of righteousness for the display of His splendor" (Isaiah 61:3). In order to become all that He wants us to be, we must remain humble and open to His Word and to the godly teaching and wisdom of others.

Are you remaining teachable? When did you last listen to or take the advice of a more experienced Christian woman?

Faith Strengthened By Trials

Greet Priscilla and Aquila, my fellow workers in Christ Jesus. They risked their lives for me. Not only I but all the churches of the Gentiles are grateful to them. Greet also the church that meets at their house

Romans 16:3-5

Read more in Acts 18:1-18; 1 Corinthians 16:19, 2; and Timothy 4:19.

Do you enjoy watching movies about super heroes? Do the scenes where they sweep down and rescue those in distress stir up your heart? Do you ever wish that you could be such a hero?

Priscilla was one woman who unwittingly became a type of hero. She and her husband, Aquila, were highly praised and esteemed by Paul because they risked their lives for him.

Priscilla and Aquila originally lived in Rome but fled when an edict was issued expelling all Jews. They arrived in Corinth where they met Paul, who had just arrived from Athens. Sharing their calling as tentmakers, they had much in common with Paul, and he chose to stay and work with them.

In Corinth, Christians faced persecution from the Jews. Priscilla and Aquilla faced real danger as they welcomed Paul and hosted church meetings in their home. When Paul left Corinth to travel to Ephesus, Priscilla and Aquila accompanied him, and it seems that they established their home and business there even after Paul traveled on.

During the months that they were in Ephesus, Paul persistently preached the gospel to the Jews, and on at least one occasion, they physically attacked him. We don't know exactly how Priscilla and her husband risked their lives for Paul, but it's possible that they somehow protected him from a hostile mob that sought to destroy everything he stood for.

This missionary couple's calling as tentmakers enabled them to move freely from one city to another. While it seems that they were always on the move, God's purpose was evident, as they were able to help establish and strengthen churches wherever they went. Their faithfulness to serve wherever God called them played a key role in the early spread of Christianity.

Though this couple faced genuine trials, they endured them together, and it seems that their faith was only strengthened by their difficulties. They lived and worked with a sense of purpose, knowing that they were called to establish, strengthen and encourage churches and often host them in their home. Persecution didn't embitter or demoralize them; it challenged them to stand firm and continue to pursue God.

Priscilla knew what she was called to do and didn't let anything — neither persecution nor her job as a tentmaker — stop her from fulfilling that goal. Today, one of the greatest challenges we face as woman is that we get so busy that we fail to prioritize the important over the urgent.

To fulfill our callings, sometimes we need to exercise wisdom and let go of the things we have willingly taken on that are filling up our agendas without being part of what God has called us to do. When people see that you are willing to serve, you will probably have more opportunities than you have time (and emotional energy) for. We need to judiciously exercise the option to say "no" and allow God to free us up to focus to serve where He has called us.

What is the main thing to which God has called you? Do you need to let go of or say "no" to any activities that are distracting you from embracing and fulfilling that calling?

A Mother's Words of Wisdom

The sayings of King Lemuel—an inspired utterance his mother taught him.

Proverbs 31:1

Charm is deceptive, and beauty is fleeting; but a woman who fears the Lord is to be praised.

Proverbs 31:30

Do you have treasured family possessions or heirlooms? Maybe a piece of jewelry or a book? There is something incredibly special about items that have family history behind them. Somehow they connect us with past generations.

My father passed his gardening book on to me — the one in which he had written notes about what he planted during each growing season. My grandmother passed on several of her baking tins to me, and when I use them, I often remember her fondly.

Of course, the real legacy of parents and grandparents (whether earthly or spiritual) are the wisdom and principles that they live, speak and teach us. We, in turn, teach their sayings or words of instruction to our children, who pass them down to our grandchildren.

One woman in history left a legacy of godly wisdom which has inspired and challenged women through the centuries. The words of Proverbs 31, King Lemuel, recorded the words that his mother taught him.

Not only did this woman teach her son about the foolishness of drinking to excess and give him other wise advice, she also left him a poem to help him when the time came to choose a wife, a woman of 'noble character.'

This mother knew that her son's choice of wife would greatly affect his happiness and impact future generations. The right choice would help him to raise godly children, and a foolish choice could bring him children who live for themselves, lacking the fear of God.

It seems likely that King Lemuel's mother had seen firsthand what happened to men who chose their wives wisely, and what befell those who made foolish choices. She may have known what had happened to King David as a result of his choices — how each of his wives contributed differently to him and to the royal household. David made a wise choice in marrying Abigail, a woman who displayed great courage and wisdom. Sometime later, he endured the tragic consequences of his lust for and adultery with Bathsheba, whom he also married.

While we often seek worldly wisdom, are we as diligent about seeking godly wisdom? Do we share and talk about the spiritual lessons that we are learning with our family and friends? In the busyness of our lives, do we take time to tell others what God is doing in and for us and how He has answered our prayers? When asked for advice, do we share the wisdom that He has taught us over the years? Those around us are quicker to follow our examples than our advice. We are only here for a short time; let's steward that time well.

When did you last share a story of how God has spoken to you, answered prayer or intervened in your life?

What do you need most from God in order to leave a Godly legacy?

Conclusion

As I read about these women's lives, I was encouraged to learn more about God's character and in particular His faithfulness. I was challenged in my own attitudes as I discovered how each woman faced and handled difficulties. I was inspired to embrace a bigger view of God in my own life, trusting Him with the detail and being more in awe of Him. I hope that your own journey of getting closer to these women has been encouraging and uplifting, as mine was.

Yet, after reading about the lives of these women, what do we learn about God, about being a godly woman and how do we apply this in our lives?

What we learn about God

We learn much about the character of God in the lives of these women. As we look at the way He interweaves the details of each life, we see that He has a perfect plan for each of their lives. As we look at these women, we see that He is faithful, coming through in their times of need. As we look at Jesus touching those around Him, we see how loving He is. As we look as He restores broken lives, we see that He is merciful and full of grace. Most of all, we see that He is loving, caring about the details of each woman's life.

We see that God is there for us. He provides the strength to handle challenging circumstances and bear difficult trials. He avenges us when we are wronged. He sustains us when life is tough. We see that when it seems that God doesn't answer prayer, He is often asking us to wait. We are reminded that God is unchangeable, that yesterday, today and tomorrow we can depend on Him to be our rock.

What we learn from these women

Each of these women displayed admirable, godly characteristics. In fact, there are over fifty characteristics displayed in at least one of these women. Each one is praiseworthy in some way, and each has something to teach us as we seek to become women who reflect God to those around us.

No woman on earth displays all of these qualities. Only one man, Jesus, lived a perfect life that showed us what God is like, yet there is one consistent characteristic exemplified in every woman whose lives we have considered.

For our answer, we return to Proverbs 31, the poem written by a godly woman and recorded for posterity by her son. We read her final words to her son:

Charm is deceptive, and beauty is fleeting;
but a woman who fears the Lord is to be praised

Psalm 31:30

What this means for you

As we seek to know what God has called us to do, fearing the Lord frees us to be just who God has called us to be, each with our unique gifts and calling. This isn't a cowering fear, but a holy reverence and awe of Him. A holy reverence for God doesn't limit us; it sets us free to be all that He has called us to be.

As we embrace a right view of a holy God, His calling to us and His unending love for us, we can know true freedom. As His sons and daughters, we discover that the fear of the Lord is truly the beginning of wisdom and the fountain of joy (Psalm 111:10). With it come many blessings, whatever our circumstances.

The Bible tells us that fearing God is the beginning of wisdom (Proverbs 9:10; Psalm 111:10), so by fearing Him we gain wisdom. As we look at these women's lives, we see many of them acting with great wisdom that can only come from God.

We watch as God guides them (Proverbs 3:6; Psalm 25:12), delivers them (Psalm 34:7), provides for them (Psalm 34:9) and fulfills their desires (Psalm 145:19). It is the fear of the Lord that is the key to unlocking such rich blessing.

As a Christian, the lives of these women are now a part of your history and heritage. Their stories have been written to encourage and inspire you. However you may feel, God has good plans and purposes for your life, He wants to use you to touch lives around you and bring Him glory.

As a child of God, adopted into His family, you are part of a heavenly lineage of truly courageous women. There is nothing God can't do with you if you allow Him!

May God bless you as you step into an exciting future as a beloved child of your Heavenly Father.

Much blessing to you,

Jennifer

Becoming A Christ-Follower

As you have been reading through these bible verses and stories, *did you wonder whether you were a Christian?*

Are you ready to become a follower of Jesus Christ? You could become one right now, by praying this simple prayer:

Father,

I am sorry for things I have done wrong.

Thank you that Jesus died for me, rose from the dead and is alive today.

Please forgive me for living life my own way.

Please come into my life and fill me with your Holy Spirit.

I accept Jesus Christ as my Lord and Savior.

I choose to follow Him today and every day.

Amen

If you have prayed this prayer, you are forgiven. Jesus has taken away all the things you have ever done wrong. You are a child of God and have been given eternal life. And you have begun your new life, strengthened by the power of the Holy Spirit.

What Do I Do Now?

- **Tell someone!** If you know other Christ-followers, tell one of them that you have prayed this prayer.

- **Find and read your Bible.** If you don't have one, get a hold of one.

- **Get involved in a local church.** A good church will help you to grow and learn as a Christ-follower.

- **Pray.** Talk to God, thank Him for the good things, forgive others and ask Him for your daily needs

About the Author

Jennifer Carter has been writing since 2004.

She has written a number of Christian titles, including:

- **Daily Readings for Difficult Days** - following her own struggle with divorce and bringing up three teenage kids as a single mom, Jennifer wrote these simple and encouraging readings to help other women who are struggling through difficult times. These daily devotions are written to women on the edge — experiencing trial, loss, suffering and pain.

- **Daily Readings, Discovering and Affirming Your Identity in Christ** — over 90 daily Bible verses containing positive affirmations for Christian women. Who does God say that I am?

By embracing God's truth in your life, it can release you to become the true woman of God who you've always dreamt (or never knew) was inside of you.

Jennifer is passionate about building the local church. She is a mother of three and a grandmother. She lives in Wiltshire, close to the cathedral city of Salisbury.

She occasionally blogs at www.hopeunlimited.com

You can find her latest books & devotionals at www.hopebooks.org

Index of Bible Women

Abigail - Whose Team Are You On?

Anna - Holding on to the Promises of God

Deborah - Time for Your Breakthrough Moment

Dorcas, or Tabitha - Fully Unwrapping Your Gifts

Elizabeth - Trusting and Being Trustworthy

Esther - Making Right Choices in Times of Crisis

Hannah - Holding Fast Through Life's Storms

Jael - Never Too Late to Make Your Choice

Jehosheba - Two Women, Two Choices

Joanna - Wealthy, Influential and Totally Sold-Out For Jesus

Jochebed - Faith for Life's Challenges & Trials

Lydia - Responding to God's Calling

Martha - Straight to the Heart of the Issue

Mary, Jesus' Friend - True Worshippers

LEGAL AND COPYRIGHT NOTICE

Whilst we endeavour to ensure that the information in the ebook is correct, we do not warrant or represent its completeness or accuracy.

We do not warrant or represent that the use of the ebook will lead to any particular outcome or result. In particular, we make no warrant of any kind relating to this ebook

To the maximum extent permitted by applicable law and subject to the first paragraph of Section [5] below, we exclude all representations, warranties and conditions relating to this ebook and the use of this ebook.

(5) Limitations and exclusions of liability

Nothing in this notice will: (i) limit or exclude our or your liability for death or personal injury resulting from negligence; (ii) limit or exclude our or your liability for fraud or fraudulent misrepresentation; (iii) limit any of our or your liabilities in any way that is not permitted under applicable law; or (iv) exclude any of our or your liabilities that may not be excluded under applicable law.

The limitations and exclusions of liability set out in this Section and elsewhere in this notice: (i) are subject to the preceding paragraph; and (ii) govern all liabilities arising under the notice or in relation to the ebook, including liabilities arising in contract, in tort (including negligence) and for breach of statutory duty.

(6) Trade marks

The registered and unregistered trade marks or service marks in the ebook are the property of their respective owners. Unless stated otherwise, we do not endorse and are not affiliated with any of the holders of any such rights and as such we cannot grant any licence to exercise such rights.]

(7) Digital rights management

You acknowledge that this ebook is protected by digital rights management technology, and that we may use this technology to enforce the terms of this notice.

(8) Governing law

This notice shall be governed by and construed in accordance with English law.